RAIDS ON
THE UNTHINKABLE

SPRING JOURNAL BOOKS
STUDIES IN ARCHETYPAL PSYCHOLOGY SERIES

Series Editor
GREG MOGENSON

OTHER TITLES IN THE SERIES

DIALECTICS & ANALYTICAL PSYCHOLOGY:
THE EL CAPITAN CANYON SEMINAR
Wolfgang Giegerich, David L. Miller, Greg Mogenson

NORTHERN GNOSIS:
THOR, BALDR AND THE VOLSUNGS IN THE THOUGHT
OF FREUD AND JUNG
Greg Mogenson

THE NEUROSIS OF PSYCHOLOGY:
PRIMARY PAPERS TOWARDS A CRITICAL PSYCHOLOGY
(FORTHCOMING, OCTOBER 2005)
Wolfgang Giegerich

RAIDS ON THE UNTHINKABLE

Freudian *and* Jungian Psychoanalyses

Paul Kugler

Spring Journal Books
New Orleans, Louisiana

© 2005 by Paul Kugler.
All rights reserved.

Published by
Spring Journal, Inc.;
627 Ursulines Street #7
New Orleans, Louisiana 70116
Tel.: (504) 524-5117
Fax: (504) 558-0088
Website: www.springjournalandbooks.com

Printed in Canada.
Text printed on acidfree paper.

Cover design by
Northern Cartographic
4050 Williston Road
South Burlington, VT 05403

Library in Congress Cataloging in Publication Data
Pending

Acknowledgments

I have been honored to present portions of this book at conferences and lectures organized by Karin Barnaby and Pellegrino D'Acierno, the Inter-Regional Society of Jungian Analysts, the C. G. Jung Society of Montreal, the Association for the Study of Dreams, the Western New York Society for Analytical Psychology, the Association of Jungian Psychology—Japan, the New England Society of Jungian Analysts, XI Seminario di Anima, the Chicago Society of Jungian Analysts, the Society of Jungian Analysts of Southern California, and the C. G. Jung Foundation of New York.

It is a source of additional pleasure that this book is being published by Spring Journal Books in the Studies in Archetypal Psychology Series edited by Greg Mogenson. Nancy Cater has worked in the background, supporting and guiding the project to completion, and Michael Mendis and Greg Mogenson have been indispensable in helping me prepare the manuscript.

I owe special thanks to those friends around the world who share my passionate interest in depth psychology and whose conversations have made this book possible: Michael Adams, Jan Bauer, Roger Brooke, Lionel Corbett, Lyn Cowan, Nancy and Thomas Dyer, Kazuhiko Higuchi, Robert Hinshaw, Harry Hunt, Thomas Kapacinskas, Tom Kelly, Peter and Lois Kugler, Stan and Jan Marlan, Alex McCurdy, David Miller, Greg Mogenson, Andrew Samuels, Gita Schulthess, Sonu Shamdasani, Dennis and Barbara Tedlock, Joe Wakefield, and Luigi Zoja.

A particular thanks goes as well to my teachers from many years ago whose presence in my memory continues to inform my work: Marie Louise von Franz, Aniela Jaffé, Charles Boer, Albert Cook, Robert Creeley, Adolf Guggenbühl, James Hillman, Norman Holland, Marshall McLuhan, Murray Schwartz, and Mark Sheckner.

Earlier versions or portions of the following chapters have been previously published: Chapter 1 as "Imagining: A Bridge to the Sublime" in *Spring 58: A Journal of Archetype and Culture* (1995), pp. 103-121 and in *The Cambridge Companion to Jung*, ed. P. Young-Eisendrath & D. Dawson (Cambridge: Cambridge University Press, 1997); Chapter 2 in *C. G. Jung and the Humanities*, ed. K. Barnaby and P. D'Acierno

(Princeton, NJ: Princeton University Press, 1990); Chapter 4 as "The Subject of Dreams," in *Quadrant: The Journal of Contemporary Jungian Thought*, XXV:2, 1992; Chapter 5 in *Fire in the Stone: The Alchemy of Desire*, ed. S. Marlan (Wilmette, IL: Chiron Publications, 1997); and Chapter 7 in *Controversies in Analytical Psychology*, ed. R. Withers (London: Routledge, 2002).

Through it all, my children—Thomas, Daniel and Christopher—have made everything possible and worthwhile.

DEDICATION

To
my son,

Christopher

Contents

Introduction	xi
CHAPTER 1: A Bridge to the Sublime	1
Originary Principles	3
A Brief History of Psychic Image	4
The Medieval View of Imaging	6
Alchemy and the Margins of Western Thought	8
The Birth of Modernism	9
Empiricism: Towards an Arbitrary Fictionalism	10
The Liberation of Imaging	12
Psychic Image in Depth Psychology	14
Psychology's Epistemological 'Object'	15
Theoretical Difference	16
Psychic Reality	17
Post-structuralism and the Linguistic Turn	18
Transcending Conscious Knowledge	19
CHAPTER 2: The Unthinkable in Depth Psychology	21
The Unknown	23
The Textuality of Psychic Life	27
Shifting Sands: Theories of Interpretation	27
Modernism's Focus on Authorial Intention	28
New Criticism: Image as Form	29
The Primacy of Structural Relations	30
Depth Psychology's Turn Towards Language	32
The Deconstruction of Authority	32
Twilight of Our God-Terms	34
An Epistemological Crisis	35
The Difference Between …	36
Deus Absconditus	37
A Few Questions	38
CHAPTER 3: The Freudian Subject	39
Id Psychology and the Oedipus Complex	41
Ego Psychology	43

Exploration of Environmental Factors	45
The Battle over the Baby	47
Psychoanalysis of Children	48
Separating from the Mother	49
Bridging Classical Psychoanalysis and Object Relations Theory	50
Differentiating Self from Other Images	52
Affectively Integrated Images	53
Borderline Personality Disorder	53
Psychology of the Self	55
Deliteralization of Theory	58
The 'Origin' of Self-Reflection	58
The Mirror Stage	59
Psychic Image and Bodily Experience	61
Constructing the Human Subject	62

CHAPTER 4: The Jungian Subject 65

Birth of the Subject	67
Death of the Subject	68
Subject and its Relation to Language	68
Imago and Psychic Text	69
The Jungian Self: A Subject Superordinate to the Ego	70
Freudian Reformulations of the Self	71
Pre-symbolic Self and Vebal Self	73
Objective and Subjective Levels of Dream Interpretation	75
Asymmetrical Mirroring	77
The Site of Reflexivity	78
Lived Experience and the Textual Realm	78
Language and Self/Other Representations	79
Inner and Outer Texts	80
Creating a Psychic Sense of Otherness	81
The Realm of the Unconscious	82

CHAPTER 5: Childhood Seduction: A Crisis in Representation 83

The Status of Psychic Images	85
Freud's Seduction Theory	88
Deliteralization of Seduction	89
The Expanded Etiology	93
Jung's Etiology	94
Confluence of History and Emotion	95

The Psychology of Rumor	98
The Empirical Perspective	100
Etiology and the Treatment of Choice	101
Theory and Types	102
Multiple Etiologies	103

CHAPTER 6: The Legacy of the Dead ... 109

The 'Ghost' of the Father	112
Somnambulism and Spirits of the Departed	112
The Holy Ghost and the Grateful Dead	114
Land of the Dead	115
Imagoes and Revenants	116
The Seven Sermons to the Dead	118
Spirits as the Exteriorization of Complexes	119
Levels of Interpretation	120
Keeping Meaning Alive	121
Individuation after Death	124
Locating Interpretation in Lived Time	127

CHAPTER 7: Psyche, Language, and Biology ... 129

Postmodernism and Social Constructivism	132
The Birth of the Mimetic Function	133
From Imago to Word: An Ontological Rupture	134
The Darwinian Revival	134
Adopting the Gene's Perspective	135
Biology and Language: A Co-evolutionary Process	137
The Baldwin Effect	139
Imitation and the Process of Replication	140
The Emergent Properties of Archetypes	141
Crossing the Animal/Human Divide	143

A Retrospective ... 145

Bibliography ... 147

Index ... 155

Introduction

Freud famously referred to what he called "the narcissism of minor differences,"[1] Jung to the antipathy of competing truths.[2] Ironically, despite these insights, Freudian and Jungian approaches to psychoanalysis have long been characterized by an historical enmity, acutely felt differences having widened into strikingly different styles of discourse. In the past, many Jungians have read the Freudian literature, but few Freudians have explored the Jungian canon. While there continues to be little referencing of Jungian texts by Freudian writers, there has been increasing receptivity on the part of Freudian analysts to opposing ideas and multi-theoretical approaches within their own tradition. Various schools of Freudian psychoanalysis have initiated professional conversations, opening up constructive dialogue between their dominant theoretical models: id psychology, ego psychology, object relations and self psychology.[3] In the Jungian world as well, we find an ever-increasing exchange of ideas taking place between the various schools of thought: classical Jungian, developmental, and archetypal.[4] While these 'conversations' have produced healthy debates *within* the Freudian and Jungian communities, there still

---

[1] Sigmund Freud, *The Standard Edition of the Complete Psychological Works of Sigmund Freud*, vol. XI, tr. J. Strachey (London: Hogarth Press, 1961), p. 199. (All subsequent references to this work, abbreviated to *SE*, will be by volume and page number). Freud returns to this reference in *SE*, XVIII, 101.
[2] C. G. Jung, *The Collected Works of C. G. Jung*, tr. R. F. C. Hull, vol. 14 (Princeton: Princeton University Press, 1971), para. 781. (All subsequent references to Jung's *Collected Works*, abbreviated to *CW*, will be by volume and paragraph number, designated by §.)
[3] See Fred Pine, *Drive, Ego, Object, and Self: A Synthesis for Clinical Work* (New York: Basic Books, 1990) and *Diversity and Direction in Psychoanalytic Technique* (New Haven, CT: Yale University Press, 1998) for an example of a multi-theoretical approach from a Freudian perspective.
[4] See Andrew Samuels, *Jung and the Post-Jungians* (London: Routledge & Kegan Paul, 1985) and *The Plural Psyche: Personality, Morality and the Father* (London: Routledge & Kegan Paul, 1989) for a Jungian multi-theoretical approach. See also, Greg Mogenson, *The Dove in the Consulting Room: Hysteria and the Anima in Bollas and Jung* (Hove, UK: Brunner-Routledge, 2003), for an example of holding the tension between the three Jungian traditions in an examination of a Freudian text by Christopher Bollas.

remains little discussion between the communities themselves.[5] In the following chapters, the two great traditions of depth psychology are brought together in an effort to rethink critically the basic tenets of psychoanalysis.

Recent trends in critical theory have worked to *deconstruct oppositions in favor of increased emphasis on the value of differences.* This has led to the development of a style of discourse that allows for a non-adversarial discussion of competing ideas and the possibility for a new type of dialogue between the various schools of depth psychology. The tradition of totalizing master narratives and absolute notions of truth and reality that so dominated the past century of depth psychology is being replaced by more modest theoretical claims based on relational models, intersubjectivity and increased openness to theoretical difference.[6] This tendency is evident in the recent movement towards *greater diversity in psychoanalytic theory and therapeutic technique.* In the past, rigidity and orthodoxy often stifled theoretical dialogue, preventing collaborative work on clinical issues. Freudian and Jungian perspectives will never dispense with or replace one another, but will, hopefully, *draw more significance from the difference between themselves.* Rather than viewing the traditions through the lens of 'either/or' logic with an emphasis on preserving a single orthodoxy, it is imperative that the psychoanalysts of every new generation critique and revise their theories, reread them through their unique subjectivity and the cultural influences of the historical moment.

While it is not possible to free ourselves completely from the unconscious influences of the traditions we espouse, if we are to avoid being completely determined by them, we must consciously

---

[5] In the 1950s, Michael Fordham and The Society of Analytical Psychology in London, England, began a project of integrating psychoanalytic concepts, especially Kleinian, with Jungian theory. Over the past 50 years, this *Klein-Jung hybrid* has produced many important clinical and theoretical contributions to depth psychology. In more recent years, *The Journal of Analytical Psychology* has sponsored a series of annual conferences bringing together leading Jungian and Freudian psychoanalysts. The following chapters are not an attempt to create another hybrid, valuable as that may be, but to work, instead, towards developing a greater openness to the *significance that lies in the theoretical differences as well as similarities.*

[6] See Christopher Hauke, *Jung and the Postmodern: The Interpretation of Realities* (London: Routledge, 2000) for an extensive discussion of the effect of critical theory and post-structuralism on contemporary depth psychology. Michael Adams's two books, *The Multicultural Imagination* (London: Routledge, 1996) and *The Fantasy Principle: Psychoanalysis of the Imagination* (Hove, UK: Brunner-Routledge, 2004) provide an extended discussion of multiculturalism in relation to Freudian and Jungian psychoanalysis.

INTRODUCTION xiii

acknowledge their place in our history. To this end, Chapter One, "A Bridge to the Sublime," examines the evolution of the concept of psychic image ('mental representation') in Western thought. From its early formulations in Greek philosophy, up through medieval onto-theology and early modernism, to the current debate over the status of image in post-structural thought, the concept has undergone a dramatic transformation. From the beginning, psychic image has been marginalized, sandwiched between two purportedly more primary ontological entities: reason and matter, mind and body, interior and exterior, subject and object. Through a careful analysis of the history of this pivotal psychoanalytic concept, Chapter One identifies an essential difference between Freudian and Jungian psychology, *a difference that reflects complementary aspects of our psychic life: reproductive and productive imaging.*

Psychoanalysis developed out of Freud's attempt to understand the role unconscious factors play in the formation of psychic life. *Unconscious* experiences were observed interfering with word association, disrupting consciousness, triggering intense affective responses, and contributing to symptom and dream formation. Chapter Two, "The Unthinkable in Depth Psychology," explores a second difference between Freudian and Jungian Psychoanalysis. Freud differentiates three distinct unconscious psychic processes: (1) preconscious thought; (2) dynamic repression; and (3) psychic processes that are inaccessible, in principle, to consciousness. The majority of the references to the unconscious in Freud's writings, however, are to *the repressed unconscious,* signifying a particular meaning or referent (ideational representative) once conscious in the individual's psyche, but no longer so.

By contrast, Jung's interest in the finitude of the human psyche led him to focus his attention on the outer limits of knowledge and those aspects of the unconscious that were, in principle, inaccessible to consciousness. Jung approached the unconscious through symbols, which, as he put it, are "the best possible expression for what is still unknown."[7] Where Freud's primary focus was on the repressed dimension of the unconscious, Jung explored the unconscious structures (archetypes) defining the finite limits of knowledge. Though different, these two aspects of the unconscious are not in opposition to each other. One focuses on the *content*

---

[7] C. G. Jung, *CW* 6 § 815, 820.

of the unconscious, while the other delineates its *structure*. Each reflects a significant dimension of the unconscious psyche.[8]

In order for unconscious experience to become conscious, it must first be *represented* in consciousness as a word, a psychic image, or 'inscribed' in flesh as a psychosomatic symptom. When 'reading' these representations, our psychic 'manuscripts,' we become, paradoxically, both 'author' and 'critic' of our own 'text.' But what are the implications of approaching our 'own' psychic images as 'other'? Who is the author of our psychic manuscripts? And by whom are they intended to be read? The answers to these questions are to be found within the history of twentieth-century textual hermeneutics. Over the past century depth psychology and literary criticism have constructed a succession of theories to interpret psychic experiences, and in the process, many important questions concerning representation, interpretation, and self-citation have been raised. Chapter Two surveys the terrain of twentieth-century critical theory with an eye towards its implications for depth psychology.

The concept of *the subject* in the history of psychoanalysis and philosophy is examined in Chapters Three and Four. What are the similarities and differences between Freud's and Jung's conception of the *human subject*? And how have these formulations changed over the past century? The subject of psychoanalysis as initially conceived by Freud has transformed dramatically over the past century. Major premises of his theory, from the role of instinctual drives and the centrality of the Oedipus complex to his technical principles, have been questioned and revised by contemporary psychoanalysis. To provide a better understanding of the contemporary Freudian notion of 'the self' and the importance of self-reflexivity in psychic formation, Chapter Three analyzes its place in the development of psychoanalytic thought, especially in relation to Lacan's divided subject and Kohut's concept of the self.

Chapter Four, "The Jungian Subject," examines how our ability to study the human subject reflexively emerges in the seventeenth century. With the appearance of Descartes's *cogito ergo sum*, the self-reflexive subject is placed for the first time at the center of Western metaphysics

---

[8] For a detailed discussion of the cultural and intellectual context behind this distinction, see Paul Kugler, *The Alchemy of Discourse: Image, Sound and Psyche*, rev. ed. (Zürich: Daimon Verlag, 2002), especially Chapter Two, "The Primacy of Structure: A Brief Genealogy."

and the human psyche, marking the transition from Medieval Scholasticism to Modernity. But with Descartes's *cogito*, depth psychology encounters the paradox that the human psyche is not only the object, but also the subject of its discipline. In Chapter Four, Jung's formulation of the ego and its relation to a superordinate *other* subject, the self, is situated within the historical development of the *cogito* in Western thought. To understand more clearly the debate between Freud and Jung, it is necessary to examine the problematic of image (reproductive/productive), meaning, and referentiality with respect to the constitution of the self-reflexive subject. A careful examination of Jung's clinical hermeneutic based on objective and subjective levels of interpretation and his asymmetrical model of self-reflection allows for a greater appreciation of *similarities and differences* between Jungian psychology, contemporary critical theory, self psychology and Lacanian psychoanalysis.

Chapter Five, "Childhood Seduction: A Crisis in Representation," returns to the theme of psychic images and the problematic of representation, this time in relation to clinical practice and the etiological significance of childhood sexual abuse. The same clinical concern that first engaged Freud and Jung has now re-emerged in professional debates. The current controversy over how to address images of child sexual abuse therapeutically oscillates between two extremes. On one end of the spectrum are the 'believers,' such as therapists specializing in multiple personality disorder, who see the patient's psychic images of abuse as deriving from traumatic childhood events that have been dissociated from consciousness. On the other end are the 'skeptics,' who doubt that any actual abuse occurred and would interpret the same psychic images as fabrications resulting from false memory syndrome.

The debate over how to interpret psychic images therapeutically brings into focus one of the central issues at the core of depth psychology, an issue that cannot simply be resolved by trying to determine what is 'real' and what is 'imaginal.' In 'memories' of childhood seduction, we witness the *dynamic interplay between productive and reproductive imaging*. Each person's psychic images *contain a certain 'truth' about his or her 'reality' and developmental history*. The point at which the clinical controversy develops is when the therapist attempts to make claims about 'reality' and 'truth' that exceed the limits of the analytic relationship. Chapter Five presents an *analysis of the implicit assumptions various theories of psychopathology import into the therapeutic relationship* to explain the significance of memory-images and fantasies of childhood sexual abuse. An examination of the ontological and epistemological assumptions operating in clinical etiologies reveals *the role played by the therapist's theory of neurosis in determining what the patient experiences as 'real' and 'true'*.

Our relationship to psychic images transforms as we move through the human life cycle. To provide a better understanding of how *lived time affects psychological understanding*, Chapter Six, "The Legacy of the Dead," examines Jung's lifelong engagement with psychic images of the dead. Beginning with the death of his parents, through the appearance of 'spirits of the departed' in his patients' pathological experiences, through the assimilation of the theoretical trope 'revenants' (spirits of the dead) in his metapsychology, and finally, to images of deceased loved ones in his final dreams, Chapter Six examines how, during the aging process, what we experience literally at one point may appear increasingly metaphorical at another. As Jung aged, the quality of his sense of lived-time changed exerting a significant influence on his understanding of the role of 'the dead' in psychic life.

The concluding chapter, "Psyche, Language, and Biology," weaves together human evolution with various themes developed earlier in the book. An intense debate has surfaced in recent years over the notion of human nature and its 'essential' aspects. The social constructivists array themselves on one side of the controversy, maintaining that language and culture play a pivotal role in 'constructing' the human psyche. Lined up on the other side are the evolutionary psychologists, who emphasize the influence of natural selection, adaptation, and human biology in the development of psychic structure. In an attempt to shed some light on the controversy, the chapter reviews the chief arguments on both sides of the language/biology debate and, in the process, proposes a new approach to understanding *how language and culture interact with biology in the natural history of the human psyche*. Whereas biological information is replicated and passed on physically to the next generation by means of genes, *language and imaging allows for the production, reproduction, and transmission of information of an entirely different sort*, psychic and cultural information, which, like biological information, can be disseminated geographically as well as through time. With the development of this psychic productive and reproductive capacity, a second means of transmitting information between individuals and across generations emerges, and the course of human evolution is forever altered.

At the start of the introduction, I indicated that this book grew out of efforts to rethink critically the basic tenets of depth psychology and, in the process, to develop a *greater appreciation of the theoretical differences and similarities* between the two great traditions of depth psychology. In the following chapters, I hope to demonstrate that constructively holding the tension between Freudian and Jungian psychoanalyses is not only theoretically possible, but even of considerable value from a clinical perspective.

CHAPTER ONE

A Bridge to the Sublime

Originary Principles

The soul never thinks without an image.[1]
—Aristotle

Imaging is an essential part of everyday life. As young children we begin to imagine long before learning to speak. Dreaming, writing, remembering, even self-consciousness would be impossible without the ability to imagine. Depth psychology developed out of an attempt to explain the role imaging plays in personality formation and psychopathology. Both Freud and Jung struggled to understand the function of 'mental representations' in psychic life. What is their origin? How are they related to the formation of identity and psychopathology? To what do psychic images refer? And how do we interpret them? For a better understanding of the importance of these questions for contemporary depth psychology, we will begin with an analysis of the historical evolution of the concept of *psychic image* in Western thought.[2]

---

[1] Aristotle, *Metaphysics*, tr. R. Hope (Ann Arbor: The University of Michigan Press, 1952), 431a 16; cf. 431b 2; 4321 8-14.

[2] The background material for this history draws primarily from three sources: Frederick Copleston, *A History of Philosophy, Volumes I-IV* (Westminster, MD: The Newman Press, 1958); Murray W. Bundy, *The Theory of Imagination in Classical and Medieval Thought*, University of Illinois Studies in Language and Literature, Vol. XII, Nos. 2-3 (Urbana, IL: University of Illinois Press, 1927); and Richard Kearney's eloquent book, *The Wake of the Imagination* (Minneapolis, MN: University of Minneapolis Press, 1988). In the history of Western thought, the psychic tendency to construct images has been portrayed primarily in two different forms: (a) as a reproductive process portraying some more primary reality and (b) as a productive process which creates original entities, images. Both meanings have attached themselves to the terms "imagination," "imagining," and "imaging." In this chapter, my usage of these three terms will follow the lead of Kearney, who acknowledges the polysemantic nature of the terms for 'imagination.' "While these different terms carry distinctive cultural and linguistic connotations, they share a common reference to the image-making power of man. This is the 'family resemblance' which underlies the diverse terms of imagination" (Kearney, p. 15). At times in this chapter, the historical or textual context will emphasize the reproductive aspect of the imaging process, while at other times the context will shift the emphasis to the productive dimension.

A Brief History of Psychic Image

> *He is a thinker; that means, he knows how to make things simpler than they are.*[3]
> —Nietzsche

The notion of *image* has undergone many transformations over the centuries, beginning with the early formulations of Greek philosophy, up through medieval onto-theology and modernism, to the current debate over the place of image in the postmodern world. The history of the concept of image begins with Plato's allegory of the cave. In the story, humans are portrayed as trapped in a cave of ignorance. The inhabitants regard the shadows on the wall as real, having no knowledge of the actual objects to which they refer. Eventually someone succeeds in escaping the cave and, in the light of the sun, views for the first time real objects.[4]

The allegory illustrates the problem of *'image' and its relation to self and reality.* Plato conceives of images (*eidōlon* or *eikōn*) as located in the external world, not as interior 'mental representations.' He characterizes their production through metaphors of 'painting' and 'figuring,' as in sculpting or creating an outer figure. Plato's theory of image begins with the assumption of an *a priori* ideal located in eternity. For example, while there are many chairs in the material world, there is only one 'form' or ideal of a chair in eternity. The various particular chairs in the material world are reflections of the 'ideal,' while images, in turn, are reproductions of the material objects. *Plato viewed images as exterior copies of the physical world, which is itself a replica of the eternal world. Images are reproductions of reproductions, not first principles.*[5]

Plato approached images with considerable ambivalence, comparing them to a 'drug,' a *pharmakon,* which may serve either as a remedy or as a poison. The image functions as a remedy when it records human experience for posterity, preventing it from

---

[3] Friedrich Nietzsche, *The Gay Science,* sec. 189.
[4] Richard Patterson, *Image and Reality in Plato's Metaphysics* (Indianapolis: Hackett Publishing, 1985), pp. 25-63.
[5] In *The Republic,* Plato defines the imagination's primary product, the image, as "an imitation of an imitation" (Book Six, esp. 510d-516c, and Book Ten, esp. 597a-599c). See also, Edward S. Casey, *Imagining: A Phenomenological Study* (Bloomington, IN: Indiana University Press, 1976), pp.15-16.

becoming lost in time. Image functions as a poison, however, when it deceives us into mistaking the copy for the original. Image becomes toxic by assuming the status of an idol.[6]

Aristotle, Plato's student, developed a different theory of image. *By shifting the area of inquiry from the metaphysical to the psychological, Aristotle located image for the first time within the human condition,* defining its source, not in eternity, but in the material world.[7] For Aristotle, *images are mental intermediaries between sensation and reason,* a bridge between the inner world of the mind and the outer material world. With Aristotle we find some of the first references to 'mental representations' (*phantasma nōtikon*). Aristotle depicts the imaging process through metaphors of 'writing,' 'draughtsmanship,' and 'drawing.' Today we still employ these metaphors when speaking of 'drawing' a conclusion or 'figuring' something out. Aristotle conceives of *images as derived from sense data*, not as an originary principle. "Nothing in the intellect except through the senses."[8]

Neither Plato nor Aristotle ever viewed imaging as an autonomous, originary process. For both, imagining remained largely a *reproductive activity.*[9] Traces of Plato and Aristotle can be found at the core of almost all subsequent Western theories of psychology. Primacy is placed either on sensation, or on atemporal cognitive structures, or on a combination of the two, as in Piaget's epigenetic model. The common thread for both Plato and Aristotle is their view of *image as a second-hand reflection of some more original source located beyond the human condition.* Imaging is a process of imitation, not creation.

---

[6] Jacques Derrida, see "Plato's Pharmacy," in *A Derrida Reader: Between the Blinds* (New York: Columbia University Press, 1991), pp. 112-143. See also, Eric Havelock, *Preface to Plato* (Cambridge: Harvard University Press, 1963), especially Chapter Two, "Mimesis."

[7] For a discussion of the appearance of the concepts of 'the mind' and 'human interiority' in the 5th century B.C.E., see Bruno Snell, *Discovery of the Mind* (New York: Dover Publications, 1982).

[8] Aristotle, *De Anima*, tr. H. Lawson-Tangred (London: Penguin Classics, 1987), 428a. See Paul Ricoeur's study of Aristotle's notion of image as mimesis in *Time and Narrative* (Chicago: University of Chicago Press, 1984), pp. 31-52. See also, Kearney, pp. 106-113.

[9] Benedetto Croce summarizes the classical view of imagining as follows: "Ancient psychology knew fancy or imagination as a faculty midway between sense and intellect, but always as conservative and reproductive of sensuous impressions or conveying conceptions to the senses, never properly as a productive autonomous activity." *Aesthetic as Science of Expression and General Linguistic,* tr. D. Ainslie (New York: Farrar, Straus, and Giroux, 1972), p. 170.

The Medieval View of Imaging

The reproductive view of imaging remained relatively intact throughout the Neo-Platonic philosophies of Porphyry, Proclus, and Plotinus, as well as up through the onto-theology of the Middle Ages. The Medieval view of imaging synthesized Hellenic ontology and Biblical theology. This onto-theological alliance served only to deepen the distrust of images. From the theological side, there was the Biblical condemnation of images as a transgression of the divine order of creation, and from the philosophical side, image was approached as a secondary copy of the original truth of being. Both the Judeo-Christian and the Greek traditions viewed imagining as a reproductive activity, reflecting some more 'original' source of meaning beyond the human condition: metaphysical forms, the physical world, or god.[10]

The Medieval understanding of imaging as represented by Augustine, Bonaventure, and Thomas Aquinas still conformed to the reproductive model of Plato and Aristotle. Throughout Medieval onto-theology, psychic image is treated as a copy, referring to a more original reality beyond itself—to a divine ideal (god) located outside the human condition.

Richard of St. Victor, a twelfth-century writer, is representative of the onto-theological view. He portrays images as 'borrowed clothing' or 'vestments' used to clothe rational ideas. Images are viewed as psychic 'garments' used to 'suit-up' reason so as to make it more presentable to the general population. Especially cautious of images, Richard of St. Victor warns that if reason becomes too pleased with its 'dress,' then imagination may adhere to reason like a skin. Were this to happen, we may mistake the artificial apparel of images for a natural possession. Richard of St. Victor warns us not to confuse our unique nature with our psychic images.[11]

---

[10] Frederick Copleston characterizes the integration of Greek ontology and Christian theology making up the Medieval onto-theological view in the following way: "The Christian world view is impregnated with the ideas derived from or suggested by Greek philosophy, so that it appears as a fusion or synthesis of Platonic elements with Christian belief. The One is the Trinity; the Logos or word became incarnate in Christ; man's likeness to God, referred to by Plato, is the work of divine grace; the human soul's return to God is not simply a solitary flight of the individual but is achieved in and through Christ as the head of the Church." *A History of Medieval Philosophy* (London: Methuen & Co. Ltd., 1972), p. 25.

[11] Richard of St. Victor, *De Unione Corporis et Spiritus* in *Patrologia Latina*, 177, 285a-289a. For an analysis of Hugo's views see Bundy, pp. 170-175; see also, Kearney, pp. 119-123.

A BRIDGE TO THE SUBLIME

In his philosophical ruminations, Hugo of St. Victor fears we may mistakenly confuse the image with our skin, our original nature. *In his warning, we begin to observe the emergence of an ambivalence in the Western psyche as to whether image is only artificial and reproductive, or whether it is actually part of our genuine nature.* The fear that psychic image might be mistakenly experienced as part of our human nature, and not simply a vestment, an artificial creation, reflects a growing uneasiness in Western thought as to the rightful place of images in relation to human nature.

As the concept of image evolves in Western thought, it brings a certain instability to the intermediary position it has been forced to occupy for the past 2000 years. The metaphysical order coming down from Plato and Aristotle has assumed certain primordial dualities: inner/outer, mind/body, reason/sensation, and spirit/matter. Image has always been sandwiched *between* these opposites. Since the beginning of Greek philosophy, these pairs have provided the foundation of Western metaphysics and have unquestioningly been assumed to support our thought structure.[12]

As Western culture evolves out of Medieval onto-theology on its course towards the Renaissance and the beginning of the modern world, these metaphysical structures begin to show signs of change. The concept of image, locked in between the fundamental dualities of Western metaphysics (inner/outer; mind/body; reason/sensation; spirit/matter), slowly begins to undergo a transformation, undermining the very metaphysical order upon which such oppositions are built. As Western thought struggles its way through Medieval onto-theology, the idea that psychic image is simply a representation of some pre-existing original, a copy of an eternal form, sensation, reason, god, or matter becomes less absolute. With the approach of the Renaissance, our relation to imaging begins to undergo a dramatic transformation. *No longer is it so certain as to whether the psychic image is a garment we put on or whether it is, in fact, our original skin!*[13]

---

[12] See Jacques Derrida, *Of Grammatology*, tr. G. C. Spivak (Baltimore: Johns Hopkins University Press, 1976), pp. 269-317; Martin Heidegger, *The End of Philosophy*, tr. J. Stambaugh (New York: Harper & Row, Publishers, 1973), p. 12; Kearney, p. 120.

[13] Bundy, pp. 173-175; Copleston, pp. 98-99; Kearney, pp. 121-123.

Alchemy and the Margins of Western Thought

The medieval view of imaging ultimately reflects its dual onto-theological nature, conforming to the fundamentally reproductive model of both its Judeo-Christian and Hellenic roots.[14] Image is still being treated as a re-presentation, a secondary mental image. As we move out of Medieval onto-theology, through the Scholasticism of the 13th and 14th centuries, toward the dawning of Renaissance humanism, a few figures just on the margins of mainstream Western thought radically begin to revise our notion of image. Paracelsus, Ficino, and Bruno develop *a new vision of imaging as a creative, transformative and originary power located within the human condition.*[15]

Copernicus revolutionized Renaissance cosmology by inverting our relation to the solar system. Traditional astronomy taught that the sun circles around the earth. Copernicus turned cosmology upside down by demonstrating that the reverse is true: the earth circles around the sun. Alchemists writing during this same time period created their own revolution in philosophy by *reversing the primary terms in our traditional theories of knowledge and image*. The presence of a 'sun' within the human universe, an inner light capable of originary powers was beginning to be intuited by alchemists and other hermetic philosophers of this period. Paracelsus asks: "What else is imagination, if not the inner sun."[16]

Bruno, a sixteenth-century Hermetic philosopher, dramatically revised the traditional reproductive view of image by going so far as to suggest that human imaging was the very source of thought itself. For Bruno, imaging precedes and, indeed, creates reason. This theoretical formulation located, for the first time, the creative force properly within the human condition, no longer in the divine, nor in eternal forms. These ideas were so radical in relation to the theological doctrines carried over from Scholastic and Medieval thought, that they were condemned as

---

[14] For Heidegger's definition of 'onto-theology' and its role in the constitution of metaphysics, see Martin Heidegger, *Identity and Difference*, tr. J. Stambaugh (New York: Harper and Row, 1969), pp. 42-75. The book consists of two little-known lectures given in 1957.

[15] Frances Yates, *Giordano Bruno and the Hermetic Tradition* (New York: Random House, 1969), pp. 68-74.

[16] Quoted in Claude-Gilbert Dubois, *L'imaginaire de la Renaissance* (Paris: Presses Universitaires de France, 1985). For an extended discussion of the psychological significance of the Copernican revolution, see Robert Romanyshyn, *Psychological Life: From Science to Metaphor* (Austin, TX: University of Texas Press, 1982), pp. 19-24. See also, Jung's essay "Paracelsus as a Spiritual Phenomenon" in *CW* 13, pp. 109-189.

heresy by the Church. As punishment for placing imaging and creativity at the center of the human condition, Bruno was burnt at the stake! Several more centuries would need to pass before it would be safe to introduce into the mainstream of Western thought the idea of *imaging as central to creativity and human nature*.[17]

The alchemical writings of this period, appearing on the fringes of Western thought, subtly begin a move beyond the metaphysics of transcendence, towards a psychology of human creativity. Up to this point, the act of creation had, for the most part, been attributed to an agency beyond the human. The typical Medieval portrait of Christ, for example, was left unsigned, an act that effaced the individuality of the painter and underscored the primacy of divine creation. *Bruno and other alchemical and hermetic philosophers of the 15th and 16th centuries began to develop the heretical idea of locating the agency responsible for the act of creation within the human condition*.[18]

The Birth of Modernism

The next significant shift in our attitude toward imaging came with René Descartes, the first modern philosopher to make a decisive break with the dominant ideas of Scholasticism (13th and 14th centuries). The ideas developed in *Meditations* (1642) are basic to the modern view of the world as being divided into subjects and objects. Working from the proposition *Cogito Ergo Sum*—I think, therefore I am—Descartes established existence on the basis of the act of a *knowing subject*, not on a transcendent god, objective matter, or eternal forms. Descartes's theory of the thinking subject signaled a major change in Western psychological understanding by *locating the source of meaning, creativity, and truth within human subjectivity*. The human mind is now given priority over objective being as well as over the divine.[19]

---

[17] Kearney, pp. 158-161. Yates argues that Bruno had a significant influence on eighteenth- and nineteenth-century German idealism, particularly that of Kant, Schelling, and Hegel.

[18] Nearly one-third of Jung's published works touches on some aspect of the hermetic and alchemical tradition. For examples, see *Psychology and Alchemy, CW* 12; *Alchemical Studies, CW* 13; *Mysterium Coniunctionis, CW* 14; and *Aion: Researches into the Phenomenology of the Self, CW* 9ii.

[19] René Descartes, *Descartes: Philosophical Writings*, tr. and ed. E. Anscombe & P. T. Geach (London: Thomas Nelson & Sons, 1954), pp. 87-152; Copleston, *A History of Philosophy*, Vol. IV, pp. 63-152.

The anthropocentric trend of the 16th and 17th centuries appears as well in the artistic realm with the emergence of 'authors' creating novels, and self-portraiture in painting begins to thrive as an instance of the new aesthetic of subjectivity.[20] The Cartesian theory of the *cogito* (the thinking subject), contains the beginnings of the modern philosophical project to provide an anthropological foundation for metaphysics. At the center of our system of thought, Descartes now locates for the first time the human subject. Descartes cut the mind free from its moorings in transcendental deities, external ideals, or the material world. *The human subject is now a first principle capable of creating a sense of meaning, certainty, existence, and truth.* However, although Descartes and his followers opened the way to modern humanism with his new theory of knowledge based on the *cogito*, his theory of image continued to subscribe to the reproductive model.[21]

Empiricism: Towards an Arbitrary Fictionalism

The next significant shift in our concept of image occurs with the empiricism of David Hume (1711-1776). Following Descartes, Hume proposed to show that human knowledge could establish its own foundation without appealing to the metaphysical realm of deities or ideals, or to the physical realm of the material world. Once reason is detached from its metaphysical scaffolding, Hume was to discover the very foundation of positivist rationalism is reduced to an arbitrary fictionalism.[22]

While Hume set out as a supporter of Locke's empiricist description of the mind as a *tabula rasa,* a blank slate, upon which the "faded impressions of the senses" are written, he ended up with a radical fictionalism, which threatened to destroy the very basis of rationalism.[23] Kearney contends that Hume pushed the reproductive view of image to its ultimate limits, declaring that all human knowledge is derived from the association

---

[20] Ernst H. Gombrich, *The Story of Art* (London: Phaidon Press, 1972), pp. 95-97.

[21] Kearney, pp. 161-163; Mary Warnock, *Imagination* (Berkeley, CA: University of California Press, 1976), p. 13.

[22] Copleston, *History of Philosophy,* Vol. V, pp. 258-395; Robert Sokolowski, "Fiction and Illusion in David Hume's Philosophy," *The Modern Schoolman* 45 (1968): 200-201.

[23] Locke's view of human nature as a *tabula rasa,* a blank slate, continues to inform contemporary theories of the mind and human nature. Steven Pinker, in his book *The Blank Slate: The Modern Denial of Human Nature* (New York: Viking Press, 2002), provides an extended critique of the problem Locke's metaphor of a *tabula rasa* brings to the study of psychology and human nature (see especially pp. 5-103).

of images and no longer needs to appeal to any metaphysical laws or transcendent entities.[24]

Hume reduces the act of knowing to a series of psychological regularities that govern associations between images. The mind is like an 'art museum' where the representations of our world are collected. Hume is concerned, not with the relation between image and world, nor between image and artist (creator), but with the laws governing the relations between images themselves: resemblance, contiguity, identity, causality, and so on. Hume focused on how images are interrelated, rather than on the laws governing reference to either the object-world or the artist-creator.[25]

While continuing to subscribe to the reproductive model of image as a mental copy of faded sensations, Hume maintains that this world of representations contained within the human subject, our inner art museum, is the *only reality we can know*. This troubling conclusion presents Hume with a dilemma: he finds himself trapped within his solipsistic museum of mental images with no way out to the 'real world.' The worlds of reason and material reality are for Hume only fictions, subjective representations with no direct connection to their referents.[26] The mental image no longer *refers to* some transcendent origin or truth, e.g., to an eternal ideal, god, or the material world. For Hume, the mental image is the only truth we can know and this means no truth at all, for he still subscribes to the *correspondence theory of truth*. If we cannot establish a correspondence between the image and its referent, we cannot establish truth. *We are left only with an arbitrary fictionalism, which we must nevertheless hold on to as if it were real.*[27]

Hume, like Aristotle earlier, now finds the human condition relating to the world through images. But the critical difference between the two is that Hume has no 'transcendent' reality beyond the images themselves. For Hume, the images do not refer to any transcendent forms (ideal or material) which give them the value of truth, and this dilemma undermines the metaphysical scaffolding which for the past 2000 years

---

[24] David Hume, *A Treatise of Human Nature* (Oxford: Oxford University Press, 1888/1976), pp. 266-267.
[25] Ned Block, ed., *Imagery* (Cambridge, MA: MIT Press, 1982), p. 82.
[26] Hume, pp. 267-268. For an in-depth discussion of Hume's arbitrary factionalism, see Sokolowski's article "Fiction and Illusion in David Hume's Philosophy."
[27] Copleston, *A History of Philosophy,* Vol. VI, pp. 404-411, 413-421; Kearney, pp.163-169; Warnock, pp. 87-88.

has supported the edifice of reality. Hume's theory of knowledge results in the following difficulty: If the 'world' we know is a collection of images and ideas without any transcendent foundations, then all we can use to establish our sense of reality are subjective fictions—foundationless images. Hume concludes: "If we embrace this principle (imagination) and condemn all refined reasoning, we run into the most manifest absurdities. If we reject it in favor of these reasonings, we subvert entirely the human understanding. We have therefore, no choice but betwixt a false reason and none at all. For my part I know not what ought to be done in the present case."[28] It is in this state of unfounded subjectivism and a deep distrust of psychic images that we find Western thought at the end of the Age of Reason. And it is in this skeptical atmosphere that 18th century philosophy prepares for a revolution in the theory of mental images.[29]

The Liberation of Imaging

In 1781, Kant stunned his colleagues by proclaiming the process of imaging (*Einbildungskraft*) to be the indispensable precondition for all knowledge. In the first edition of his *Critique of Pure Reason*, he demonstrated that both reason and sensation, the two primary terms in most theories of knowledge up to this point, were *produced, not reproduced, by imaging*.[30] This radical shift was already under way with Hume's arbitrary fictionalism, but for Hume, images were still reproductive. Kant's revolution turned on two important points: first, he re-conceives the process of imaging as both *productive and reproductive*; and second, he locates the synthetic categories and their process of imagining *transcendent* to reason.[31] Platonic metaphysics had located

---

[28] Hume, pp. 267-68; Kearney, p. 167. For a discussion of Hume's theory of knowledge, see John Richetti, *Philosophical Writing: Locke, Berkeley, Hume* (Cambridge, MA: Harvard University Press, 1983), pp. 183-263.

[29] Robert Avens, *Imagination is Reality* (Dallas: Spring Publications, 1980), pp. 13-14; Kearney, pp. 155-188; Warnock, pp. 35-41. In *Madness and Civilization*, Foucault documents the invention of the mental hospital during the Age of Reason as a social and political means for incarcerating mental images and non-reason.

[30] Kearney's reading of Kant's theory of the transcendental imagination expands on Martin Heidegger's analysis of the imagination presented in *Kant and the Problem of Metaphysics*, tr. J. S. Churchill (Bloomington, IN: Indiana University Press, 1962), pp. 144-148.

[31] In his book, *Imagining*, Casey describes the productive and reproductive aspects of Kant's theory of imagination in the following fashion: "As transcendental in status, the *productive* imagination is a necessary condition for all imagining—indeed, for the perceptual experience as well. As empirical, it is 'formative' and is crucial in the creation of art. But Kant also recognized a *reproductive* imagination which operates by associating sensory contents given to it in intuition" (p. 132).

the originary principle in an eternal transcendental realm, beyond the human mind, while medieval onto-theology located it in god. Kant, struggling with the arbitrary fictionalism resulting from dispensing with all transcendental foundations, *established a new ground, this time within the human condition itself, but transcendent to reason.* Two hundred years earlier, a similar view of psychic images had led to Bruno's being burnt at the stake. Kant's extraordinary formulation turned the entire hierarchy of traditional epistemology on its head by demonstrating that pure reason could not arrive at the objects of experience *except through the finite limits established by imaging. All knowledge is subject to the finitude of human subjectivity.* Simply put: *Imaging is the indispensable precondition of all knowledge.*[32]

After Kant, psychic images could no longer be denied a central place in our theories of knowledge, art, existence, and psychology. With this epistemological shift, mental image ceases to be viewed as a reproduction, or a reproduction of a reproduction, and now *assumes the role of ultimate origin* and creator of meaning and our sense of reality. Images create our consciousness, which then provides the illumination of our world. Where image had previously been approached through the metaphor of a *mirror reflecting the world*, Kantian metaphysics re-conceives imaging through the trope of the *magic lantern* providing the illumination for our knowledge of the world.[33]

The relationship between reason and image has come a long way since early Greek thought. As we enter the 19th century, a more peaceful rapport between the two begins to be established. Kant's liberation of image spawned, in the 19th century, powerful new movements in art and philosophy. In England, the new romanticism celebrated the liberation of image from the grip of reason (Descartes's *cogito*) in the works of Blake, Shelley, Byron, Coleridge, and Keats. The celebration continued, as well in France through the works of Baudelaire, Hugo, and Nerval. And in philosophy, German idealism developed in the writings of Fichte and Schelling. Each movement re-emphasized the importance of image in the human condition, but as with so many new movements, the emphasis went too far. Confronted with the Industrial Revolution, the devastation of nature, and the exploitation of the individual by unbridled capitalism, the idealism of romantic humanism

---

[32] Avens, pp. 14-17; Kearney, pp. 155-188; Warnock, pp. 13-71.
[33] See Meyer H. Abrams, *The Mirror and the Lamp: Romantic Theory and the Critical Tradition* (Oxford: Oxford University Press, 1971), pp. 160-168.

gave way to a more down-to-earth sense of the synthetic powers of imaging in the existential philosophies of Kierkegaard and Nietzsche.[34]

Psychic Image in Depth Psychology

> *I am indeed convinced that creative imagination is the only primordial phenomenon accessible to us, the real Ground of the psyche, the only immediate reality.*[35]
>
> —C. G. Jung

As we enter the 20th century, one hundred years after Kant, another transformation in our concept of image is about to occur. Freud had already begun to explore the recesses of the human mind through an analysis of psychic images. Dreams, fantasies, and memories were carefully examined in an attempt to understand how 'mental representations' are involved in our sense of self and reality, personality development, and symptom formation. While these were new and puzzling questions for psychiatry, the problem of imaging was by no means new in the history of Western thought. In the early years of depth psychology, Freud expanded our understanding of the human psyche through his formulation of Oedipal dynamics, the theory of drives, and id psychology. His theory of imaging, however, continued to subscribe to the reproductive model, approaching psychic images as *representations* of either drives, wishes, or historical events.

In his effort to understand the role of image in mental life, Jung took a different approach, opting instead, to view imaging as an *autonomous activity of the psyche, capable of both production and reproduction*.[36] Earlier, Kant had revolutionized philosophy, counteracting Hume's arbitrary fictionalism by establishing imaging as a transcendent ground within

---

[34] Jung was significantly influenced by Nietzsche. Between the years 1934 and 1939, Jung conducted a seminar on Nietzsche's *Zarathustra*, the transcription of which totaled more than ten volumes. The seminar was edited by James L. Jarrett and published in an abridged form in two volumes by Princeton University Press under the title *Nietzsche's Zarathustra: Notes of the Seminar Given in 1934-1939* (1988). See also, Liliane Frey-Rohn, *Friedrich Nietzsche* (Einsiedeln: Daimon Verlag, 1988) for an extensive discussion of the influence of Nietzsche on Jung.

[35] C. G. Jung, *C. G. Jung Letters, Vol. I: 1906-1950*, ed. G. Adler, tr. R. F. C Hull, Bollingen Series XCV:1 (Princeton, NJ: Princeton University Press, 1973), p. 60.

[36] In *The Alchemy of Discourse*, I used the terms *productive imaging* and *reproductive imaging* to differentiate better these two primary aspects of psychic imaging. See Jung, *CW* 7 § 121-140.

the human mind. Kant's categories provided the *a priori* structures necessary for reason itself. The subtle implications of Kant's *Critique of Pure Reason* Jung extended to the realm of depth psychology, positing archetypes as the *a priori* categories of the human psyche.

> One could also describe these forms as categories analogous to the logical categories which are always and everywhere present as the basic postulates of reason. Only, in the case of our "forms," we are not dealing with categories of reason but categories of the imagination.[37]

In attempting to differentiate the categories of the imagination, Jung extends Kant's critique of pure reason to an analysis of the finitude of the human psyche, thereby shifting the epistemological 'object' of depth psychology from sexuality to psychic image. The theory of archetypes (the categories of the psyche) refocuses the epistemological inquiry from the objects of experience (things) to an analysis of our modes of knowing them, i.e., the transcendental (*a priori*) functions of the mind.[38]

Psychology's Epistemological 'Object'

The formation of a new psychology has been described by the historian, Sonu Shamdasani, as consisting of *a parallel construction of the new theory and its 'object' of study*. The constitution of an epistemological 'object' upon which to establish a new psychology involves taking an aspect of human nature and imbuing it with universality, ahistoricity, and essentialist attributes.[39] The founding of psychoanalysis as a psychology began with Freud's constituting sexuality as an epistemological 'object.'

---

[37] C. G. Jung, *Psyche and Symbol* (New York: Anchor Books, 1958), pp. 292-93.

[38] In recent years, Freudian psychoanalysts have rediscovered Kant and the importance of establishing the epistemic status of the human psyche. See Mauro Mancia & Luigi Longhin, "Kant's Philosophy and its Relationship with the Thought of Bion and Money-Kryle," *International Journal of Psychoanalysis* 81.6 (2000): 1197-1211; Wilfred R. Bion, *Learning from Experience* (London: William Heinemann, 1962); Wilfred R. Bion, "A Theory of Thinking, Part II of the Psycho-analytic Study of Thinking," *International Journal of Psychoanaysis* 43.2 (1962): 306-10; Salomon Resnik, *L'esperienza psicotica* (Turin: Bollati Boringhieri, 1986); Salomon Resnik, *Spazio mentale: sette lezioni alla Sorbona* (Turin: Bollati Boringhieri, 1990).

[39] Sonu Shamdasani, "Psychologies as Ontology-Making Practices: William James and the Pluralities of Psychological Experience," *William James and the Varieties of Religious Experience*, eds. J. Carrette, R. Morris, & T. Sprigge (London: Routledge, 2002); see also, Bruno Latour, "The Historicity of Things," *Pandora's Hope: Essays on the Reality of Social Sciences* (Cambridge, MA: Harvard University Press, 1999), pp. 145-73.

Through an analysis of desire in relation to dreams, symptoms, parapraxes and early childhood memories, Freud developed a comprehensive theoretical narrative capable of explaining and treating a patient's psychological symptoms. Over the next century, Freudian psychoanalysis underwent a succession of shifts in its epistemological 'object,' resulting in the development of new theories and treatment models: *id* psychology, *ego* psychology, *object relations* psychology, *self* psychology and *relational* psychology. As each new epistemological 'object' has come into clinical focus, the result has been the theoretical articulation of *different and 'essential'* aspects of the human psyche.

Theoretical Difference

The theoretical difference between Freud and Jung developed over the epistemological 'object' of choice. Where Freud emphasized the primacy of sexuality, Jung focused on image and the finitude of human knowledge, theorizing that the psyche possesses its own synthetic categories, analogous to the logical categories of reason.

> The original structural components of the psyche are of no less surprising a uniformity than are those of the body. The archetypes are, so to speak, organs of the prerational psyche. They are eternally inherited forms and ideas which have no specific content. Their specific content only appears in the course of the individual's life, when personal experience is taken up in precisely these forms.[40]

Jung's use of the metaphor of bodily 'organs' sets up a biological analogy, emphasizing the inherited *potential* to form epistemic structures.[41] Knowledge of an individual's psychic experience is 'organ'-ized in a particularly human way and might be compared to the 'stomach'

---

[40] Latour, p. 293. Bion also drew on Kant in his formulation of 'the pre-conception': "The preconception may be regarded as the analogue in psychoanalysis of Kant's concept of 'empty thoughts'" (*Learning from Experience*, p. 306).

[41] In 1978, Noam Chomsky used the same 'organ' metaphor in articulating his approach to the study of the human mind: "I have been suggesting that we pursue the study of mind—that is, the principles that underlie our thoughts and beliefs, perceptions and imagination, the organization of our actions, and the like—much as we investigate the body. We may conceive of the mind as a system of 'mental organs,' the language faculty being one. Each of these organs has its specific structure and function, determined in general outline by our genetic endowment, interacting in ways that are also biologically determined in large measure to provide the basis for our mental life." "Language and Unconscious Knowledge," in *Psychoanalysis and Language*, ed. Joseph Smith (New Haven, CT: Yale University Press, 1978), p. 27.

A BRIDGE TO THE SUBLIME

in relation to 'food.' The specific content of human experience is 'metabolized' according to the psyche's synthetic categories, subjecting all *psychological experience* to the *finitude* of the human psyche.

Psychic Reality

The psyche consists essentially of images.[42]
—C. G. Jung

The psyche and its capacity to create images Jung locates as a mediating agency between the inner world of ideas and the outer world of things.

> ... [A] third, mediating standpoint is needed. *Esse in intellectu* lacks tangible reality, *esse in re* lacks mind. Idea and thing come together, however, in the human psyche, which holds the balance between them. What would the idea amount to if the psyche did not provide its living value? What would the thing be worth if the psyche withheld from it the determining force of the sense-impression? What indeed is reality if it is not a reality in ourselves, an *esse in anima*? Living reality is the product neither of the actual, objective behavior of things nor of the formulated idea exclusively, but rather of the combination of both in the living psychological process, through *esse in anima*.[43]

By shifting the epistemological focus from sexuality to psychic image, Jung formulated a radically new understanding of *psychic reality*. No longer is 'reality' to be found in god, eternal ideals, or matter, but instead, the *experience* of reality is located within the human condition as a function of psychic imaging: "The psyche creates reality every day. The only expression I can use for this activity is *fantasy*. ... Fantasy, therefore, seems to me the clearest expression of the specific activity of the psyche. It is, pre-eminently ... [a] creative activity."[44] The inner *and* outer worlds of an individual come together in psychic images, giving the person a vital sense of *a living connection to both worlds*. "Fantasy it was and ever is which fashions the bridge between the irreconcilable claims

---

[42] Jung, *CW* 8 § 618.
[43] Jung, *CW* 6 § 77.
[44] Jung, *CW* 6 § 78.

of subject and object."[45] The *experience* of reality is a product of the psyche's capacity to imagine and is the 'essence' of being human. With this ontological shift, mental image ceases to be viewed as a reproduction and now assumes, following Kant, the role of ultimate origin and creator of meaning and of our *sense* of existence and reality.

Post-structuralism and the Linguistic Turn

As we enter the 21st century, the debate over the role of imaging continues to flourish, but with a new twist. In the past fifty years, a revolution has occurred in language philosophy with a shift in emphasis from the role of image to the role of language in human understanding. The new continental philosophers, especially Derrida and Foucault, have developed a radical critique of Western thought, focusing on the age-old problem of establishing a ground, an originary principle, for the *act of interpretation*.[46] Throughout history, we have used such metaphysical universals as truth, reality, self, center, unity, origin, archetype, or even author to ground the act of interpretation. The new twist Derrida brings to this old problem revolves around making explicit the language-locked nature of verbal acts of interpretation. All theories of knowledge are housed in language and work through figures of speech, which render them ambiguous and indeterminate. The reader of any *text* is suspended between the literal and metaphoric significances of the text's 'root' metaphors and is thus thrown into the semantic indeterminacy of the text.[47]

Derrida's deconstruction of the linguistic foundations of Western theories of knowledge is a logical extension of Hume's empiricist critique of imaging. Just as Hume pushed the reproductive view of image to its ultimate limits by forgoing any appeal to transcendent foundations, so Derrida pushes the reproductive theory of language to its ultimate limits. By eliminating any appeal to transcendent entities (universals), Derrida focuses on the relation between words, rather than referentiality. The *difference* between words becomes the primary point of reference, rather than the word's relation to the author (hence, 'the death of the author'),

---

[45] Jung, *CW* 6 § 78.

[46] Derrida, *Grammatology*; Michel Foucault, *Madness and Civilization: A History of Insanity in the Age of Reason*, tr. R. Howard (London: Tavistock Publications, 1967); Michel Foucault, *The Order of Things: An Archaeology of the Human Sciences* (New York: Random House, 1970); and Christopher Hauke, *Jung and the Postmodern: The Interpretation of Realities* (London: Routledge 2000).

[47] Derrida, *Grammatology*, especially "The Originary Metaphor," pp. 169-180.

or some other transcendent object of reference. Dismantling the metaphysical scaffolding of language results for Derrida in the same troubling dilemma Hume had encountered earlier. Once we dispense with linguistic referentiality (the implicit assumption in the 're-productive' metaphor) we find ourselves trapped in the solipsism of language—unable to transgress the text. The Derridian text no longer refers to some transcendent origin, meaning, or truth, and consequently *post-structuralism finds itself caught in a postmodern version of Hume's arbitrary fictionalism.*[48]

Transcending Conscious Knowledge

As the status of 'transcendent terms' has been called into question, so too have the essential elements of human nature. Concern about the 'existence' of shared human properties is an old philosophical issue, one that dominated Medieval onto-theology in the form of the debate between nominalism and realism. The nominalist argued that there is no connection between words and things (referents), while the realist treated language as signifying a reality beyond itself. This old debate, which has re-emerged as a result of the post-structural critique of referentiality in language, is expressed today in the following terms: constructionist vs. universalist coupled with difference vs. sameness. Advocates of constructionism, a postmodern form of nominalism, typically appeal to the 'sociological,' the 'historical,' or the 'intersubjective' categories to demonstrate that universal attributes are constructed in time, rather than given as metaphysical realities. But in the process, the constructivists frequently, but implicitly, *universalize their root metaphors: 'the social,' 'the historical' or 'the intersubjective'.* Even if the hallmark of universalizing, *the* definite article, is removed, or singular nouns are pluralized, some degree of universalizing is still involved in the constructivist project as the price of linguistic formulation.[49]

---

[48] Derrida, *Derrida Reader*. See "Speech and Phenomena," pp. 14-16 for Derrida's reading of Hume's fictionalism.

[49] A closer examination of the universalism-sameness/constructivism-difference opposition reveals that they are not as dichotomous as initially thought. While "universalism" and "sameness" are often grouped together as one pair and "constructivism" and "difference" another, upon closer analysis this *ideal* pairing fails to hold in practice. For example, any specification of a group simultaneously argues for difference from other groups and sameness within the specified group. The grouping "women" requires both *difference* from other groups (e.g. men, animals, etc.), and *sameness* within the group specified (ignoring sexual preference, race, class, and so on).

By placing psychic imaging as the mediator between idea and thing, we open up a new understanding of its role in creating our sense of psychic reality. Jung's formulation of psychic image as a bridge between the inner world and the outer world is located in his *Psychological Types*[50] just after an extended discussion of the Medieval debate between nominalism and realism. Jung formulates his view of imaging as a mediating third position, *esse in anima,* between what today would be called constructivism and essentialism. Psychic images point beyond themselves to *both* the historical particulars of the world around us, as well as to the mind and metaphysics. Psychic images signify something that consciousness cannot quite grasp, the as yet unknown depths, transcendent to subjectivity. And this depth is to be found in both the world of things and the world of ideas. What psychic images signify cannot be determined precisely, either by appeal to a difference or a universal. While the *significance* of the image remains elusive, it does, however, induce consciousness to think beyond itself, not to interpretations presented by either archetypalists with their appeal to divinities, nor by constructivists with their appeal to history, nor even by evolutionary psychologists with their appeal to genetics, but to a knowing that cannot be designated *a priori*. Perhaps the most important function psychic images perform is to aid the individual in transcending conscious knowledge. Psychic images provide a bridge to the sublime, pointing towards something unknown, beyond subjectivity.

Whether difference or sameness is accentuated seems to be a matter of focus: to predicate some attribute of the category 'human being' necessarily foregrounds commonality, whereas to do so with 'Asian-Americans' will contrast them (for the moment) with both the white American majority, as well as other minority groups. How we construe the *markings* of sameness or difference will vary enormously, in part according to our relation to the group being designated and also according to whether we *believe* the markings are constructed or given, i.e., universal. See Diana Fuss, *Essentially Speaking: Feminism, Nature and Difference* (New York: Routledge, 1989).

[50] Jung, *CW* 6.

CHAPTER TWO

The Unthinkable in Depth Psychology

When I prepared this little talk for you, it was early in the morning. I could see Baltimore through the window and it was a very interesting moment, because it was not quite daylight and a neon sign indicated to me every minute the change of time; and naturally there was heavy traffic; and I remarked to myself that exactly all that I could see, except for some trees in the distance, was the result of thoughts, actively thinking thoughts, where the function played by the subjects was not completely obvious. ... The best image to sum up the unconscious is exactly Baltimore in the early morning [emphasis added].[1]
—J. Lacan

I am conscious that I am moving in a world of images and that none of my reflections touches the essence of the unknowable.[2]
—C. G. Jung

The Unknown

Depth psychology began with Freud's attempt to factor into the equation of human nature 'unknown' background elements participating in the formation of psychic life.[3] 'Unthought' experiences were observed interfering with consciousness, disturbing memory and word association, activating intense affective responses and contributing to symptom and dream formation. These 'unknown' factors have become known as the unconscious. But what is actually *meant* by 'the unconscious'? Is it a psychic realm topographically located

---

[1] Jacques Lacan, "*Sur un terrain en friche*: Liminal note," lecture delivered at Johns Hopkins University, 1966, transcribed and translated by R. Macksey, in *Lacan and Narration*, ed. R. C. Davis (Baltimore: Johns Hopkins University Press, 1983), p. 845.

[2] C. G. Jung, *The Collected Works of C. G. Jung*, tr. R. F. C. Hull, vol. 11 (Princeton: Princeton University Press, 1971), para. 556. All subsequent references to Jung's *Collected Works* (abbreviated to *CW*) will be by volume and paragraph number, designated by §.

[3] Sigmund Freud, *The Standard Edition of the Complete Psychological Works of Sigmund Freud*, vol. XIV, tr. J. Strachey (London: Hogarth Press, 1961), p. 166. All subsequent references to this work (abbreviated to *SE*) will be by volume and page number.

'below' consciousness? Is it a psychopathology characterized by a disturbance of consciousness? Is it the representation of biological drives? The real? Or the unknown? Why has so much been written about the 'X', the unknown element in the equation of individuality?

In his classic paper entitled, "The Unconscious," Freud differentiates three ways in which psychic processes can be unconscious: (1) preconscious thought (latent); (2) dynamically repressed (ideational *representatives* of instincts are barred from consciousness); and (3) aspects of the psychic process that are in principle inaccessible to consciousness. Most of Freud's references in the *Standard Edition* are to the repressed unconscious, although he clearly indicates that the repressed and the unconscious are not identical: "Everything that is repressed must remain unconscious; but let us state at the outset that the repressed does not cover everything that is unconscious. The repressed is a part of the unconscious."[4] Freud's 'repressed unconscious' refers to a particular meaning or referent (ideational representative) not conscious in the individual's psyche. For example, the 'unconscious' may refer to a repressed wish, a drive, a complex, an internalized object, or a derivative from the bi-personal or intersubjective field.

Jung, on the other hand, focused more, though not exclusively, on those aspects of the psychic process that are in principle inaccessible to consciousness. His interest in the finitude of the human psyche drew his attention to the outer limits of knowledge. Jung's classic definition of a symbol reflects this epistemological sensibility: A symbol is the best possible expression for something essentially unknown.[5] Archetypes present the same epistemological barriers found in Piaget's (1973) cognitive unconscious and Chomsky's deep structures.[6] In a paper on "Language and Unconscious Knowledge," Chomsky defines the epistemological limits of unconscious knowledge. He writes:

---

[4] Freud, *SE* XIV, 166-169. See also, "Introduction," *Psychoanalysis and Language*, ed. J. H. Smith (New Haven, CT: Yale University Press, 1978), pp. ix-xxx.

[5] Jung, *CW* 7 § 492: "The symbol is not a sign that disguises something generally known. Its meaning resides in the fact that it is an attempt to elucidate, by a more or less apt analogy, something that is still entirely unknown or still in the process of formation."

[6] Noam Chomsky, "Language and Unconscious Knowledge," in *Psychoanalysis and Language*, ed. J. Smith (New Haven, CT: Yale University Press, 1978), pp. 3-44.

> Even Freud's evocation of the unconscious was not, I believe, accompanied by far-reaching questions of the accessibility in principle of the products of the mind[7] ... More explicit rejection of accessibility appears in remarks by C. G. Jung. He writes that 'there is little hope of our ever being able to reach approximate consciousness of the self, since however much we may make conscious there will always exist an indeterminate amount of unconscious material which belongs to the totality of the self.' Jung's archetypes are 'empty and purely formal' structures; each is a 'possibility of representation which is given a priori,' 'an irrepresentable, unconscious, pre-existent form that seems to be part of the inherited structure of the psyche.'"[8]

While Freud and Jung worked in analytic practice with both aspects of the unconscious, each tended to construct theoretical formulations that emphasized one aspect of the unconscious more than the other. To illustrate the two different uses of the term 'unconscious,' consider the following stories.

The first is found in the eighteenth book of the *Koran* and begins with Moses meeting Khidr (the 'Green One') in the desert. The two wander together and Khidr expresses his fear that Moses will not be able to witness his deeds without judgment and indignation. Khidr tells Moses that if he cannot trust and bear with him, then Khidr will have to leave. Moses agrees. After a short time they come upon a poor fishing village where Khidr sinks the fishing boats of the villagers. Moses sees this and is upset, but remembers his promise and says nothing. A short time later, they arrive at a decaying house of two pious young men, just outside the wall of a city of non-believers. Khidr goes up to the city wall, which is falling down, and repairs the wall rather than the house of the two believers. Again Moses is disturbed by Khidr's actions but says nothing. The story continues in this way until finally Moses sees something so intolerable that he can no longer hold back making a comment on the significance of the events—an interpretation. This causes Khidr to leave. But before his departure, Khidr explains why he acted as he did. In the first instance, pirates were on their way to steal the boats and by sinking them, Khidr actually saved the boats from being stolen. In the second instance, by rebuilding the wall of

---

[7] Chomsky, p. 29.
[8] Chomsky, p. 31.

the city of non-believers, Khidr actually saved the young men from ruin. Their life savings, hidden in the wall of the city, were about to be revealed and stolen. As Khidr leaves, Moses realizes that his judgment had been too hasty and Khidr's actions, which he initially interpreted as negative, were in fact not so. The 'true meaning' of Khidr's actions are at first unconscious. Moses is unconscious of the significance of Khidr's behavior and only near the end of the story does Moses and the reader become conscious of the significance of the events.

I would like to contrast this story with a second one in which we find the same recontextualization taking place, but this time without an unconscious 'transcendent' meaning or referent. The second story presents a very different relation to 'not knowing.' It is an old Taoist story about a farmer who has a son and a horse. One day the farmer goes outside to find that his only horse has run away. It is a small village and the neighbors hear about this and come to visit that evening, telling him what a terrible thing it is that has happened. The farmer listens to them, thinks for a while, and responds, "I don't know." The next week the horse runs up into the mountains and takes up with a herd of thirty wild horses. After running with them for a few weeks, the farmer's horse leads the wild horses back to the corral. The farmer goes out and finds he now has thirty-one horses and closes the gate. Word gets out about the new horses and that evening the neighbors come to visit him. They tell him how wonderful it is that he now has thirty-one horses. The farmer thinks for a long time and replies, "I don't know." The following day his only son goes out to tame the horses. He climbs on the first horse and is thrown, breaking his leg so he cannot work. The neighbors hear about this and come over for a visit that night. They tell him how terrible it is that his only son has broken his leg and cannot work. The farmer thinks about this for a while and responds: "I don't know." The next day the country goes to war and the man in charge of conscription arrives to draft the son to go and fight on the front line where he will probably be killed. He finds the son has a broken leg and tells the boy he does not have to go to war. The neighbors hear about this and come over that night and tell the farmer how wonderful it is that his son does not have to go to fight in the war. And the farmer responds: "I don't know."

The stories highlight different aspects the unconscious. Both are similar in their relativizing of the original events through recontextualization. In the first story there is a personification (Khidr) who 'knows' (signifies) the unconscious meaning of the events, whereas in the second story no such personified transcendent knowledge exists. Instead, we have a protagonist resisting the neighbors' tendency to fix a specific interpretation to an event.

The Textuality of Psychic Life

> *The unconscious is neither primordial nor instinctual; what it knows about the elementary is no more than the elements of the signifier.*[9] —Jacques Lacan

The problem of defining 'the unconscious' in more than abstract terms is difficult, if not impossible. By its very nature, *the unconscious defies representation* and eludes the language we speak. The unconscious is an experience our conscious mind cannot comprehend. For unconscious experience to be apprehended by the conscious mind, it must first be *represented* psychically in consciousness as a word or a psychic image, or inscribed in flesh as a psychosomatic symptom. These representations in consciousness constitute *the textuality of our psychic life*. When reading and analyzing these psychic manuscripts we are, paradoxically, both author and analyst of our own text. But what is implied in reading our 'own' psychic images as 'other'? How is an interpretation of the unconscious possible? *Who* is the author of our psychic text? *Who* is the intended reader? And to what extent are these questions about the problematics of representation and interpretation the effect and function of language itself? To answer these questions we need to turn to the field of textual hermeneutics.

Shifting Sands: Theories of Interpretation

The history of interpretation is a history of *the psyche's struggle to understand itself in time*. Depth psychology over the past one hundred years has constructed a succession of clinical hermeneutics used

---

[9] Jacques Lacan, "The Insistence of the Letter in the Unconscious," *Structuralism*, ed. J. Ehrman (New York: Anchor Books, 1970), p. 130.

therapeutically to interpret patients' psychic experiences. Patients expect their psychic experiences to be taken seriously by analysts as legitimate and meaningful. Psychologists desire, as well, that their theory of therapeutic interpretation be accepted and legitimated. When patients and therapists work together toward developing a therapeutic understanding of dreams, symptoms and suffering, both parties are unconsciously influenced by the interpretative models currently being legitimated on the cultural and scientific level. To gain a better understanding of how this background process of authentication influences our understanding of the human psyche and transforms over time, we will review some of the critical interpretative models that have dominated Western culture since the inception of depth psychology.[10]

Modernism's Focus on Authorial Intention

Over the past 100 years, a revolution has occurred in the field of textual interpretation. In the early part of the 20th century, the Modernist School of literary theory was the dominant model for textual interpretation. The Modernist approach was guided by the assumption that a close scholarly reading of original manuscripts, biographies, and histories would lead to an understanding of the 'true' interpretation of the text in question. This form of 'empirical' criticism imagined the subjectivity of the interpreter to be a transparent, focusable lens through which a detached consciousness could view a stable text. The reader, as detached observer, focused primarily on an analysis of the *author's intention as the means for deciding which of many possible meanings was the 'true' interpretation of the text.*[11]

The Modernist hermeneutic was guided by the implicit assumption that the 'true' meaning was to be found in authorial intention. What the creator intended in the process of composing the text is its 'real' meaning. In depth psychology, during this same period, a similar interpretive attitude was cultivated in the interpretation of dreams. The analyst, as detached observer, 'objectively' viewed and interpreted the patient's dream text through a knowledge of the patient's psychiatric history, psychodynamics, and free associations.

---

[10] Edward Shorter, *From Paralysis to Fatigue: A History of Psychosomatic Illness in the Modern Era* (New York: The Free Press, 1992), pp. 2-25.

[11] William K. Wimsatt & Monroe C. Beardsley, *Literary Criticism: A Short History* (Lexington, KY: University of Kentucky Press, 1957).

Through an 'objective' analysis of the clinical material, it was thought to be possible to discover the *patient's unconscious intentions* and, therefore, the 'true' meaning of the dream text. This approach is particularly characteristic of classical Freudian psychoanalysis.

New Criticism: Image as Form

In the 1940s and 50s, the Modernist Movement gave way to a new approach known as 'New Criticism.' Drawing heavily upon the earlier work of the modernist writers, the New Critics shifted the focus of textual analysis from *history and content* to *form*, emphasizing *imagery* as the constituent of form itself. New Criticism approached a text as a complex system of *forms* analyzable at different levels of generality. For example, a poem was analyzable on multiple levels—from the specific components of a poetic image or line, through the poem's genre, to that genre's place in the system of literature. The strategy adopted by the New Critics emphasized the autonomy of the text and the presence of meaning within it, *shifting the reader's focus from authorial intention to a close examination of the text itself.* The previous use of historical and biographical information about the author was now considered to be problematic and guilty of committing the 'intentional fallacy.' How could anyone really know the intention of Milton or Blake? A text reveals its own significance without needing historical or biographical information to illuminate it.

The New Critics, especially Cleanth Brooks, William Wimsatt, and Monroe Beardsley, produced a powerful methodology. They focused the reader's *attention on the text*, its conflicts and resolutions, especially emphasizing the *unity* and *coherence* that inevitably seemed to emerge out of these internal tensions. This new style of reading attempted to disclose the existence of collective human patterns, not confined to particular times, places, and biographical facts. Where modernism reflected many of Freud's original interpretative attitudes, the New Critics echo many of Jung's: *the autonomy of the psyche, the focus on the emerging image patterns, the move to the deeper collective themes, the discovery of paradox and reconciliation, and the belief in the ultimate unity and coherence of the psyche.* In recent years, however, these newer styles of interpretation have also been called into question and, in the process, many important issues have emerged. Not only is the author's intention a disputable point, but the text's autonomy, unity, and ability to reveal some referential truth have also been challenged.

The Primacy of Structural Relations

The most significant school of interpretation to emerge after Modernism and the New Critics was Structuralism, a methodology that drew heavily on the work of Ferdinand de Saussure, especially his *Course in General Linguistics*. Saussure's most significant contribution to linguistics is his shift in focus away from the historical, etymological, and referential aspects of linguistics, to a focus on how language functions as a collective system of signs. For Saussure, the basic units of language—sound and meaning, signifier and signified—are defined systemically through internal *differences*, rather than by some *correspondence* to the material world or to etymological history. To demonstrate the importance of structural relations, as opposed to the previous focus on the substantive and historical aspects, Saussure suggests we compare the system of language to a game of chess. Historical and material changes in a chess piece do not affect the *meaning* of the piece. Rather, the meaning of each piece is generated by the *role the piece plays and how it is used in relation to the other pieces*. If, for example, we use fifty-year-old ivory chessmen, instead of new plastic ones, the change in material substance has no effect on the system of structural relations, the rules of the game. If, however, we change the number of chessmen, we alter the structure or 'grammar' of the game. Saussure concluded that "language is a form not a substance." Meaning is a product of structural relations, not material history.[12]

Saussure envisioned a new science called semiology. Using structural linguistics as its model, semiology presented the possibility of describing all cultural phenomena through a study of the life of signs within society. From Saussure's structural linguistics, a new interpretative vision emerged in which representational qualities (i.e. the sign's ability to mirror nature or the human psyche) became much less important than how *words and images work as a system of structural relations*.

In 1949, Lévi-Strauss applied the structuralist insights to psychoanalysis, reformulating the Freudian topographical model of the mind. The phenomenon that Freud had earlier referred to as the

---

[12] Paul Kugler, *The Alchemy of Discourse: Image, Sound and Psyche*, rev. ed. (Zürich: Daimon Verlag, 2002), pp. 41-55.

'unconscious' Lévi-Strauss now subdivided into two distinct aspects. The first he referred to as the *subconscious* and the second retained the name *unconscious*. In his revised formulation, the subconscious consisted of psychic 'substances,' memories and imagoes collected in the course of an individual life, while the unconscious was conceived of as 'empty' and limited to the imposition of structural laws. Lévi-Strauss's reformulation is very similar to Jung's earlier subdivision of the unconscious into a personal aspect composed of imagoes and a collective aspect consisting of archetypal structures.[13] The unconscious, for Jung and the structuralists, functions like an empty stomach, structurally digesting the individual psychic substances taken in during the course of the person's life. Lévi-Strauss describes his reformulation of the Freudian unconscious this way:

> One could therefore say that the subconscious is the individual lexicon where each of us accumulates the vocabulary of his personal history, but that this vocabulary only acquires signification, for ourselves and for others, in so far as the unconscious organizes it according to the laws of the unconscious, and thus makes of it a discourse. ... The vocabulary is less important than the structure.[14]

The similarity between Lévi-Strauss's structural model and Jung's archetypal model can be seen in the following description of the function of the archetype, written by Jung some 20 years earlier.

> It is necessary to point out once more that archetypes are not determined as regards their content, but only as regards their form and then only to a very limited degree. A primordial image is determined as to its content only when it has become conscious and is therefore filled out with the material of conscious experience. Its form, however, as I have explained elsewhere, might perhaps be compared to the axial system of a crystal, which as it were, performs the crystalline structure in the mother liquid, although it has no material existence of its own. ... The archetype in itself is empty and purely formal, nothing but a *facultas praeformandi*.[15]

---

[13] Kugler, *Alchemy of Discourse*, pp. 73-85.
[14] Claude Lévi-Strauss, *Structural Anthropology* (New York: Anchor Books, 1967). See especially Chapter II: "Structural Analysis in Linguistics and Anthropology."
[15] Jung, *CW* 9i § 155.

Depth Psychology's Turn Towards Language

In 1953 Jacques Lacan, one of the most influential French psychoanalysts, adopted Lévi-Strauss's revised structural model, introducing into psychoanalytic terminology a tripartite system for ordering the personality: the 'real,' the 'imaginary,' and the 'symbolic.'[16] The object-as-such attempting to be known Lacan refers to as the 'real,' while the representation of that object, the psychic imago, constitutes the 'imaginary.' On the other hand, the symbolic order performs a purely structural function, organizing psychic representations into meaningful units. Psychic images are structured by the symbolic order analogous to syntax organizing lexical elements into semantically meaningful units. Lacan shifted the foundation of psychoanalysis from biology to language, replacing traditional drive theory with structural linguistics. The importance of Lacan's contribution to theories of textual interpretation is in his emphasis on the process through which personality development is dependent on and invented in a matrix of culturally determined symbols (signifiers) making up our textual environment. The personality develops in and through a collective system of linguistic signifiers which structures the unconscious like a language.[17]

The Deconstruction of Authority

The structuralist project focused primarily on the representational realm and worked toward developing *an objective science of interpretation capable of revealing the symbolic structures underlying all psychic narratives.* By the late 1950's and early 1960's, Roland Barthes, Claude Lévi-Strauss, and Jacques Lacan had extended Saussure's semiological approach to anthropology, literature, culture, and psychoanalysis. Structuralism maintained enormous popularity throughout the late 1960s and 1970s until it gradually began to self-destruct from within. In one of his late works, Barthes began to question the structuralists' tendency to catalogue all the world's narratives within a single set of archetypal structures. He wrote:

> We shall, they thought, extract from each tale its model, then out of these models we shall make a great narrative structure,

---

[16] Jacques Lacan, "*Le Symbolique, l'Imaginaire et le Réel,*" Conférence à la Société Française de Psychanalyse, July 8, 1953 (unpublished).

[17] Jacques Lacan, *Ecrits,* tr. A. Sheridan (New York: W. W. Norton & Co., 1977).

which we shall reapply (for verification) to any one narrative; a task as exhaustive as it is ultimately undesirable, because the text thereby loses its difference.[18]

In abandoning the search for *structural similarities and refocusing the reader's attention on differences,* Barthes was partially responding to a new continental philosophy rooted in the writings of Hegel and Nietzsche, and epitomized in the work of the French poststructuralist philosopher, Jacques Derrida.[19] The new mode of interpretation, referred to as deconstruction, called into question our Western metaphysical tendency to ground the act of interpretation in 'absolutes' such as *truth, reality, self, center, unity, origin,* and even *author.* Our Western style of thought has been committed to a belief in some 'ultimate' presence, truth, or reality with a fixed unimpeachable meaning. This fixed meaning acts as the unquestionable 'ground' from which to interpret or explain all the other elements in our text. For example, a theory of dream interpretation might be grounded in such absolutes as sexuality, self, wish, center, wholeness, death, energy, the analytic frame, intersubjectivity and so on. *For these 'absolutes' to perform their interpretative function, they must transcend the very system of thought they seek to explain.*

But how is this transcendence accomplished? How do we bootstrap the clinical material to a therapeutic interpretation? This is accomplished by positing the 'absolute' as coming temporally before or after (or both) the phenomenon being interpreted. The meaning of the dream is then either causally derived from, or teleologically moved toward, this first principle. If the therapist is theoretically committed to *a priori* ultimates, the meaning of the dream comes about through a reduction to absolutes such as drives, the family, archetypes, biochemistry, the previous day's experiences, childhood traumas, and so on. Notice how all of these absolutes are located in the past. The dream interpretation might also be grounded in a posited absolute in the future. For example, the dream might be interpreted as moving toward and referring to ultimates such as the Self, wholeness, unity, soul, or death. For these first principles to perform their explanatory function, they cannot be implicated in the very system of thought and language they are being used to explain;

---

[18] Roland Barthes, *The Pleasure of the Text,* tr. R. Howard (London: Macmillan & Co., 1976).
[19] Jacques Derrida, *Of Grammatology,* tr. G. C. Spivak (Baltimore: Johns Hopkins University Press, 1976).

nor can their meaning have the same semantic status as the other meanings within the system. Their semantic status must be something like the 'meaning of meaning' or the 'metaphor of metaphors.' *These transcendental 'god'-terms function as the linchpins for our Western theories of clinical interpretation.*

Twilight of Our God-Terms

These unquestionable 'absolutes' are not the eternal structures we once thought them to be, but increasingly appear to be, in part, *linguistic by-products* resulting from the acquisition of language. The metaphorical meaning of a transcendental term cannot be separated from its literal meaning, even if that is the author's declared intention. No linguistic concept is exempt from the metaphorical status of language. No mode of discourse, not even the language of science, can be only literal. All writing is by its very nature ironic, simultaneously literal and metaphoric.

Through the process of constructing a method of interpretation, even one 'purely' phenomenological and descriptive in nature, *certain terms in the text will be literalized and given a privileged ontological position around which the other elements in the linguistic system will revolve and to which they will refer.* At times, one term in this category of privileged elements is seen as the 'origin' of all the other terms. For example, in Jungian psychology the 'Self' performs this function, while in classical Freudian theory it is performed by the concept of 'drives.' Notice, however, that once the 'origins' question is evoked, it is difficult to think of an origin without wanting to further ask about the origin of the posited origin. *Just here we experience how language has subtly trapped us inside the logic of the 'origins' metaphor, unconsciously elevating the term to a transcendental status that now attempts to account for all the other terms.* The originary, explanatory principle explains everything, except itself, and is therefore not the ultimate explanatory principle. This same problem exists for absolutes given teleological status, such as wholeness, unity, Self, soul, energy, and even death.

The dissolution of absolutes in our theories of knowledge had already begun at the end of 19th century with Nietzsche's declaration that "God is dead." Nietzsche wrote:

> WE HAVE KILLED HIM—you and I. All of us are his murderers. But how have we done this? How were we able to

drink up the sea? Who gave us the sponge to wipe away the entire horizon? What did we do when we unchained the earth from the sun? Whither is it moving now? Whither are we moving now? Away from all suns? Are we not plunging continually? Backward, sideward, forward, in all directions? Is there any up or down left? Are we not straying as through an infinite nothing? … God is dead. God remains dead. And we have killed him.[20]

Nietzsche's declaration of the Death of God is a philosophical gesture to make conscious the role played in our system of thought by 'transcendental signifiers.' The process of factoring time into a phenomenological understanding of our theories of interpretation discloses that the grounds of Western knowledge, the 'horizon,' the 'sea,' the 'sun,' as well as our textual god-terms—truth, meaning, center, author, unity—all *lapse into a temporal regress or progress*. For example, Freud and the modernists attempted to explain the meaning of a text through authorial intention, while Jung and the structuralists later tried to account for meaning and interpretation through unconscious psychic structures. These solutions, however, do not account for the 'authority of the author' or the 'structurality of structure.' These explanations simply posit the author or structure as existing in time prior to the emergence of the text, psyche, or system of thought.

An Epistemological Crisis

This critique of Western epistemology leads to the realization that all conscious knowledge, as well as our theories of knowledge, work through figurative structures which render them ambiguous and indeterminate. The reader of any text is suspended between the word's literal and metaphoric significance, unable to choose definitively between the two meanings, or meaning and referent, and is thus thrown into the semantic indeterminacy of the text.

The movement from structuralism to post-structuralism is a dramatic shift from seeing the text as a closed entity with definite, decipherable meanings, to seeing the text as irreducibly plural, oscillating between literal and figural significances which can never be fixed to a single

---

[20] Friedrich Nietzsche, *The Gay Science*, in *The Portable Nietzsche*, ed. and tr. W. Kaufmann (New York: Viking Press, 1968), p. 97.

center, essence, or meaning. Contrary to the structuralists' desire to construct an objective, interpretative science, it has become increasingly apparent that theorists cannot create a terminology transparent to their truths. We have come to realize that language of any sort, be it literary, philosophical, clinical, or scientific, does not allow for a transparent view to the so-called empirical world. *Our theories of interpretation have no location outside of language, neither objective nor empirical, and can never be a ground, only a mediator.*

The modernist project of developing an objective hermeneutic imagined the reader's subjectivity as a transparent focusable lens through which a detached consciousness could view the content of a stable text. The empiricist idea continued through stucturalism, except that the focus of the 'detached' observer shifted from the content of the text to its structure. This view has changed dramatically with the advent of post-structuralism. As the Cartesian subject-object dichotomy begins to dissolve, so too does the traditional image of the separation between reader and text, consciousness and language, psyche and the world. No longer can we view texts as objects with a stable meaning, for, in the end, it is language that speaks in texts, in all its swarming, polysemic plurality, not the author or reader. When we think, speak, or write, it is impossible for our consciousness to escape the power and influence of the metaphors, the 'dreams' haunting the interior of our language. *The lens of consciousness is always clouded by the tropes (figures of speech) of the text that we are reading or writing.*

The modernist-structuralist idea of a detached observer is being replaced by the idea of an intersubjectivity where the images in the text interfuse with and alter the lens of the viewer reading the text. We not only read texts, but *we read the world through texts*. It is precisely this realization that has undermined our epistemological confidence in the authority of our transcendental signifiers. *The more we attempt linguistically to account for the authority of these ultimates, the more the absoluteness in our god-terms begins to deliteralize, dissolve, and disappear.*

The Difference Between ...

In speaking or writing about the psychic phenomena between conscious and unconscious, between 'I' and 'me,' we become caught up in the *semantic dynamics between the literal and the figural*. All discussions about the psyche will be caught up in and unconsciously structured by the tropes in our speech.[21] These metaphors unconsciously structure the perceptions of our patient's psychology, 'highlighting' certain aspects and 'filtering out' others. If we forget this, the privileged metaphors in our theories begin unconsciously to structure our way of psychologically thinking and speaking. When this happens, the rhetorical structures, the 'dreams' in our theories, begin producing unconsciousness in our clinical practice.[22] Today it is as important for us to perform an analysis on the 'dreams' in our theoretical texts, as it was a century ago for Freud and Jung to perform a dream analysis on their patient's psychic text. It has taken over one hundred years for us to realize that 'dreams' inhabit texts as well as the night.

Ultimately, as long as we speak and write, we cannot escape these rhetorical 'powers.' Language is always a metaphor for something else, even if that 'something else' is itself. Self-reflection is made possible, but escape is not. This is the great value and limitation of language. While we cannot escape the powers of language, we can, as responsible psychologists, at least become more conscious of the rhetorical processes 'informing' our texts, as well as our lives. These textual 'informants' are the figures in our speech being taken literally.[23]

Deus Absconditus

The realization that our clinical grounds are not as absolute as we once thought does not lead to a radical relativism, nor to a nihilism. It leads, instead, to a psychological realism based upon the awareness that all systems of clinical interpretation gain their authority through a grounding in a god-term, a transcendental 'ultimate.' But this 'ultimate' is no longer so absolute, so ultimate. In therapeutic analysis we must still, on one level, believe in our god-term, and use it as if it were the ultimate explanatory principle. But on a deeper level, we also know it is not. And it is precisely this deeper level of awareness that prevents our psychological theories from becoming secular

---

[21] A. John Soyland, *Psychology as Metaphor* (London: Sage Publications, 1994).
[22] Donald Spence, *The Freudian Metaphor: Toward Paradigm Change in Psychoanalysis* (New York: W. W. Norton & Co., 1987).
[23] George Lakoff & Mark Johnson, *Metaphors We Live By* (Chicago: University of Chicago Press, 1980).

religions and differentiates professional debates from religious idolatry. *The ultimate ground of depth psychology is not a known god-term, but the ultimately unknowable, the unconscious itself. And this is the absolute ground which gives authority to all schools of depth psychology.*

A Few Questions

Our theories of interpretation have come a long way over the past century and in the process many important questions concerning representation, self-citation, and interpretation have been addressed. When these same problematics are applied to depth psychology, the following questions are raised: (1) How does a self become self-reflexive? (2) How does psychology develop a theory of interpretation that is itself self-conscious, i.e., a theory capable of consciously carrying an awareness of its own figural aspects and implicit ontological and epistemological assumptions—its own unconsciousness? (3) Is the psychic image performing a reproductive or productive function, or both? How do we responsibly hold the tension between these two aspects of imagining? (4) When interpreting a dream, which meaning is given primacy in our theory and practice: The literal meaning (the objective level of interpretation), the metaphoric (the subjective level of interpretation) meaning, or both? What are the therapeutic, psychological, political, and ethical implications of privileging only one meaning or arranging the two meanings hierarchically? (5) To what does the psychic image refer? The outer world? The inner world? Both worlds? Or is it self-referential? (6) What is the relation between the discourse of analytic theory and the discourse of the analysand? Is analytic theory a form of meta-discourse—a language about another language which can rise above its object of study to a point from which it can peer down and 'objectively' examine the analysand's psyche? Is this kind of meta-position ever possible in depth psychology? (7) How much, if any, of the patient's dream text does the reader-analyst write (construct) in the process of clinical interpretation? (8) Is the Self, a wish, the soul, biochemistry, or some other 'transcendent ultimate' the author of the dream? Or does the dream text have no author? On what principle do we 'ground' the act of therapeutic interpretation? (9) And finally, what is the 'subject' of depth psychology?

CHAPTER THREE

The Freudian Subject

It is clear, I am sure, that my view of what constitutes the analytic is not a classical or a Kleinian position. I think that each of the schools in some respects polemicizes a single feature of analytic life. Each Freudian should also be a potential Kohutian, Kleinian, Winnicottian, Lacanian, Bionian, as each of these schools only reflects a certain limited analytic perspective.[1]

—Christopher Bollas

The subject of psychoanalysis has been dramatically reconceptualized and transformed over the past century. The major premises of Freud's theory—the role of instinctual drives, the centrality of the Oedipus complex, the primacy of sexuality and aggression—as well as his technical principles—the systematic frustration of the analysand's wishes, analytic neutrality, regression to an infantile neurosis—have all been significantly called into question and transformed by contemporary psychoanalysis. In this chapter, we will trace the development of psychoanalytic theory and clinical practice, from its origin in Freud's work to the current diversity of analytic models.

Id Psychology and the Oedipus Complex

At the beginning of the 20th century, Freud's focus was on the Oedipus complex and the vicissitudes of id psychology. The central issues of human life were packaged into the resolution of critical childhood relationships occurring between the ages of five and six. The year 1923 marked a critical turning point in the history of psychoanalysis, second in its significance only to 1897, when Freud expanded his

---

[1] Christopher Bollas, *Forces of Destiny: Psychoanalysis and Human Idiom* (London: Free Association Books, 1989), p. 99.

seduction theory and first articulated the Oedipus complex.[2] In 1923, Freud published *The Ego and the Id*, introducing his new structural model of the psyche and setting the stage for the development of ego psychology. The same year, a number of other significant texts were also published: Sándor Ferenczi's *Thalassa*, Otto Rank's *The Trauma of Birth*, Georg Groddeck's *The Book of the It*, and *The Development of Psychoanalysis* co-authored by Rank and Ferenczi. Where *The Ego and the Id* refocuses psychoanalysis on the intrapsychic structures of the ego, superego and id, Ferenczi, Rank, and Groddeck (an obscure new analyst) are busy turning the lens of depth psychology in a different direction, towards a two-person psychology which factors the analyst's subjectivity into the therapeutic equation and emphasizes the mutuality of the therapeutic relationship.

The year 1923 is also the year Freud was diagnosed with cancer. While a number of Freud's early followers—Jung and Rank in particular—had attempted to analyze him, only Ferenczi and Groddeck offered to take him into analysis after the onset of his cancer. In 1909, during the transatlantic crossing to the Clark University Conference, Freud refused to enter into a mutual analytic relationship with Jung and Ferenczi. This refusal in part contributed to his conflict with Jung: "I could tell you more, but I cannot risk my authority."[3] On February 26, 1926, Ferenczi wrote to Freud: "Perhaps this is the occasion on which I can say to you that I find it actually tragic that you, who endowed the world with psychoanalysis, find it so difficult to be—indeed, are not at all—in a position to entrust yourself to anyone."[4] That both Ferenczi and Groddeck each independently offered to take Freud into analysis at this critical time is testimony to their compassion and concern for the founder of psychoanalysis. Freud did not accept either offer for fear of jeopardizing his authority.

Groddeck, the director of a sanatorium in the German town of Baden-Baden, first wrote to Freud in 1917 to thank him for his work and apologize for critical remarks he had previously published on psychoanalysis. Of particular interest to Groddeck was the extension of

---

[2] Peter L. Rudnytsky, *Reading Psychoanalysis: Freud, Rank, Ferenczi, Groddeck* (Ithaca, NY: Cornell University Press, 2002), p. 141.
[3] C. G. Jung, *Memories, Dreams, Reflections*, ed. Aniela Jaffe, tr. R. & C. Winston, rev. ed. (New York: Vintage Books, 1963), p. 158.
[4] Sigmund Freud & Sándor Ferenczi, *The Correspondence of Sigmund Freud and Sándor Ferenczi, Vol. 2, 1914-1919*, eds. E. Falzeder & E. Brabant, tr. P. T. Hoffer (Cambridge, MA.: Harvard University Press, 1996), p. 250.

psychoanalysis to the treatment of physical disease. Freud went on to appropriate Groddeck's concept of the "It" (Es) in his new structural model of the psyche, defining the "Id" (Es) as the mental region that is foreign to the ego. Freud wrote to Groddeck on June 18, 1925, "In your It (Es) I naturally cannot recognize my civilized, bourgeois id (Es) stripped of mysticism. Still, you know, mine is derived from yours."[5] While Freud borrowed his key metapsychological concept from Groddeck, *The Ego and the Id* charted a course for psychoanalysis diametrically opposed to Groddeck's theory. Where Freud's 1923 book set the agenda for the future of ego psychology, Groddeck's *The Book of the It* established his place in psychoanalytic history as the progenitor of relational psychology.[6]

Ego Psychology

The introduction of Freud's structural model of the psyche based on three agencies began the shift away from drive theory and the Oedipus complex towards ego psychology and identity theory. This theoretical reorientation became especially pronounced after Freud's death in 1939 and lasted up through the late 1960s and early 1970s. Prior to the publication of *The Ego and the Id*, Freud used the term 'ego' in a rather loose, unsystematic way to refer to the conscious collection of ideas from which the repressed unconscious is separated. After 1923, however, Freud applied the term more precisely to represent one of the three agencies making up his new model of the mind. The structural model shifts the location of psychic conflict from the tension between conscious and unconscious to the struggle between the three internal agencies. The main function of the ego in Freud's new tripartite structure is to relate to reality and through the creation of defenses to channel and control inner drives in relation to outer reality.[7]

Freud's daughter Anna played a crucial role in the development of ego psychology and child analysis. In 1936, she published *The Ego and Mechanisms of Defense*, which became the handbook for ego psychology. For the first time, she defines the "proper" analytic attitude as "neutral,"

---

[5] Freud & Ferenczi, p. 152. Groddeck's "It" is theoretically more akin to Jung's and Kohut's concepts of the "Self" than Freud's "Id".

[6] See Peter L. Rudnytsky, ed., *The Psychoanalytic Vocation: Rank, Winnicott, and the Legacy of Freud* (New Haven, CT: Yale University Press, 1991) for a careful mapping out of the historical precursors to intersubjectivity and relational psychology.

[7] For an extended discussion of the significance of the year 1923 in the history of psychoanalysis, see Rudnytsky, *Psychoanalytic Vocation*, pp. 141-206.

adopting an evenhanded approach to all three agencies of the psyche. Anna Freud significantly expanded the clinical focus of psychoanalysis by differentiating the various defense mechanisms of the ego, locating them along a developmental continuum. Through a careful study of the pervasiveness of the ego's processes and defenses, Anna Freud established the ego as a primary object of analytic inquiry. Her work expanded the scope of depth psychology from psychopathology to character styles, further opening up to psychoanalysis the study of the normal functioning of the personality already begun by Jung with his research in Word Association Experiments and his book on *Psychological Types* (1921).[8] The shift from id to ego psychology resulted, as well, in significant changes in technique. More direct engagement of the patient was permitted with less emphasis on revealing unconscious secrets and free association. Analysts began paying greater attention to the assessment of psychic structure, the development of ego functions and the analysis of defense mechanisms.

The importance of ego psychology was further established with the publication of Heinz Hartmann's book, *Ego Psychology and the Problem of Adaptation* (German, 1937; English, 1958). Hartmann's shift in emphasis from id to ego functions had a dramatic effect on the subsequent history of psychoanalysis.[9] Where Freud had focused on "conflict," especially conflicts between consciousness and the repressed unconscious, or conflicts between sexuality and aggression, or conflicts between the id, ego and superego, Hartmann turned his attention to what he called the "conflict-free" functions of the ego. Freud had earlier perceived the ego's functions as embedded in psychic conflict and forged out of tensions and frustration. Hartmann's new developmental theory radically challenged the primacy of conflict in psychic life.

Drawing on Darwin's theory of evolution, Hartmann argued that humans were designed by evolution to fit physically, as well as psychologically, into their natural environment. Freud's self-absorbed baby, full of erotic and aggressive conflicts, was reimagined by Hartmann as a more 'conflict-free' baby with intrinsic ego potentials and functions which develop naturally in a healthy environment. While continuing

---

[8] C. G. Jung & F. Riklin, "The Associations of Normal Subjects," *Studies in Word Association*, tr. M. D. Eder (New York: Moffat, Yard & Co., 1919), pp. 8-172.

[9] Fred Pine, *Drive, Ego, Object, & Self: A Synthesis for Clinical Work* (New York: Basic Books, 1990), pp. 27-34.

to value the classical psychoanalytic view of conflict, Hartmann undertook a study of nonconflictual adaptive child development through a careful differentiation of ego operations, their origin, function, and relationships with one another. The shift from id to ego psychology resulted in several significant changes. The clinical emphasis moved from analysis of the repressed unconscious and conflict resolution to an emphasis on the functions of the ego, its defense mechanisms and problems of adaptation. Where Freud had been preoccupied with the intrapsychic dynamics of drives, Hartmann began to explore the role of the environment in psychic development. A change occurred as well in the metaphors used to characterize the analytic process. Freud had evoked metaphors of "battles", "wars" and "conflicts," while ego psychology spoke of "working alliances" and "therapeutic partnerships."[10]

Exploration of Environmental Factors

The shift in emphasis from intra-psychic conflict and drives, to the exploration of environmental factors took another dramatic step in 1945 with the publication of Réne Spitz's *Hospitalism*, a clinical study documenting a tragedy in a South American orphanage.[11] Having witnessed many epidemics of infectious disease spreading from infant to infant, the well-intentioned administrators at the orphanage constructed a new facility in which every child had its own immaculately maintained crib. The staff was instructed to wash their hands and to put on new sterilized gloves before working with a different infant. While everything possible was done to prevent infection and malnutrition, the babies suddenly began to withdraw socially, became apathetic, listless, and despondent, and often failed to thrive. Spitz observed that while the babies were kept clean and well fed, they had been deprived of a loving caregiver's touch and affection. Lack of any ongoing *nurturing interaction* took an enormous toll, both on the children's emotional development, as well as on their physical growth. As this *emotional deprivation* extended beyond three to four months, motor retardation

---

[10] For an analysis of the role played by theoretical metaphors in paradigm shifts, see Donald Spence, *The Freudian Metaphor: Toward Paradigm Change in Psychoanalysis* (New York: W. W. Norton & Co., 1987), pp. 17-70; See also, Stephen Mitchell & Margaret Black, *Freud and Beyond* (New York: Basic Books, 1995), pp. 34-38.

[11] René A. Spitz, "Hospitalism: An Inquiry into the Genesis of Psychiatric Conditions of Early Childhood," *The Psychoanalytic Study of the Child,* ed. R. S. Eissler, vol. I (New York: International Universities Press, 1945).

occurred and eye coordination deteriorated. Thirty-seven percent of the babies died before the end of their second year, and those who survived to their fourth year suffered acute developmental disturbances in their ability to walk, stand, or talk.[12]

Spitz's study documented the results of emotional neglect, one of the most severe forms of stress. The orphan children's failure to experience the touch of a soft, warm body and a smiling face in front of them created a form of emotional starvation. The study graphically demonstrated that whatever inborn psychological potentials the human baby has, their realization is dependent upon ongoing emotional connectedness with another person. Earlier Freud had heralded *emotional abstinence* (not gratifying drives) as a stimulant to ego development that *forces the critical turn away from primary narcissism towards reality*. Spitz's study of "failure to thrive" infants, however, dramatically demonstrates that emotional abstinence on the part of the primary caregiver is potentially deadly to the infant.

The tragedy at the South American orphanage raised important questions about how the outer environment affects the development of the child's inner life. Hartmann had already begun to shift the focus of child development studies from intrapsychic conflicts to the interpersonal dynamics between the infants and caregivers. For the development of ego functions, such as language acquisition, object comprehension, and perception, certain environmental factors are necessary. If food and other physical needs are not the *crucial nurturing factors*, then what exactly does psychic involvement with a nurturing person involve? Spitz concluded that providing only for a baby's physical needs is not sufficient for normal development. In his efforts to understand how the outer environment affects the development of the child's inner life, Spitz adopted a theoretical position halfway between Freud's id psychology and a new theory of object relations. Hartmann had earlier described the infant's psyche as "undifferentiated," implying that at birth the ego, superego, and the basic drives are not differentiated. Spitz expanded the psychoanalytic focus on early life by describing the infant as initially *both* "undifferentiated" intrapsychically and "non-differentiated" interpersonally—the infant is born psychologically embedded with its mother.

---

[12] René A. Spitz, "Hospitalism: A Follow-up Report on the Investigation Described in Volume I," *The Psychoanalytic Study of the Child,* ed. R. S. Eissler, vol. II (New York: International Universities Press, 1946). Spitz introduced the term 'anaclitic depression' to describe the attachment disorder occurring in these infants.

How does a baby psychically and physically differentiate from its mother and grow into an autonomous child? Spitz would spend the rest of his life trying to find the answer to this question and, in the process, discovered many of the critical developmental signposts or "organizers of the psyche," the infant passes during the process of individuation. The smiling response at three months, the first recognition of the mother's face accompanied by anxiety in response to a stranger's face at eight months, and the acquisition of "no" at about fifteen months, comprise the first three psychic organizers. Spitz spent his professional life documenting, often on film, how the newborn develops out of an undifferentiated state with the primary caregiver to become an autonomous child, independent of the maternal environment.[13]

The Battle over the Baby

During the 1920s and 30s, Melanie Klein published a series of papers that significantly altered the clinical approach to the treatment of children. Klein was born in Vienna in 1882 and, after brief stays in Budapest and Berlin, settled permanently in London. Already by the late 1920s, Klein and her followers in London began to clash with the more classical Freudians. This conflict began to divide the psychoanalytic world into the "London School" and the "Viennese School." In 1938, when the war forced Anna and Sigmund Freud to move to London, the stage was set for "The Battle over the Baby."[14]

Shortly after Freud's death, the British Psychoanalytic Society conducted a series of highly charged discussions over the differences in theory and technique between the two schools of psychoanalysis. Anna Freud and her followers argued that young children could not be analyzed because their egos were too weak, unable to tolerate interpretations of instinctual conflicts. Focusing primarily on ego development and the analysis of defenses, Anna Freud studied the Oedipal period of development between five and six years of age. Rather than analysis, Anna Freud recommended a quasi-educational approach to young children.

---

[13] René A. Spitz, *The First Year of Life* (New York: International Universities Press, 1965).
[14] Phyllis Grosskurth, *Melanie Klein: Her World and Her Work* (New York: Alfred A. Knopf, 1986). See "Part Five: The Controversial Discussions, 1942-1944," pp. 279-362.

Psychoanalysis of Children

The Kleinian approach to children was quite different, focusing instead on much earlier stages of development, especially the pre-Oedipal years of two to three. Klein contended that young children are analyzable and can handle analytic interpretations, as long as the child's play is interpreted like an adult analysand's free associations. Through her child analyses, Klein claimed to have discovered archaic fantasies of incestuous union, precursors to the Oedipus complex, and terrifying images of self-punishment attributed to early aspects of the superego. The debates over technique and theory resulted in a split of the British Psychoanalytic Society into three groups. The first group, the *Classical Freudians,* included followers of Sigmund and Anna Freud and tended to dominate the International Psychoanalytic Association and American psychoanalysis up to the 1980s. The second group, the *Kleinians*, consisted of Melanie Klein and her followers. The third group, the *Independents* (or *Middle Group*), included W. Ronald Fairbairn, Donald Winnicott, Michael Balint, John Bowlby, and Harry Guntrip.[15]

In the 1940s and 50s, the Kleinians and the Independents began to develop a new theoretical understanding of the role psychic images play in interpersonal dynamics known as *object relations theory*. With the shift from id and ego psychology to object relations, the clinical focus turned to the role mental representations play in the formation of psychic structure and psychopathology, especially pre-Oedipal disorders.[16] The main analysts writing in this new tradition were Klein, Bion, Guntrip, Winnicott, and Fairbairn.

In 1943, Fairbairn, an important pioneer in object relations theory, stunned the British Society by reading the following statement at a members' meeting:

> ... [I]n my opinion the time is now ripe for us to replace the concept "phantasy" by a concept of an "inner reality" peopled by the ego and its internal objects. These internal objects should be regarded as having an organized structure, an identity of their own, an endopsychic existence and an activity as real within the inner world as those of any object in the outer world. To attribute such

---

[15] Grosskurth, pp. 359-360.
[16] Pine, pp. 183-197.

features to internal objects may at first seem startling to some, but, after all, they are only features which Freud has already attributed to the Super-ego.[17]

Fairbairn's epoch-making statement carried deep resonances with Jungian metapsychology, especially his revised notions of 'phantasy' and 'inner reality' in relation to Jung's concept of 'psychic reality.' These resonances did not go unnoticed. In London early in the 1950s, Michael Fordham, a child psychiatrist and Jungian analyst, initiated an experiment later termed *the Klein-Jung Hybrid*. The Society of Analytical Psychology began to forge together the clinical and theoretical sensibilities of Jung and Klein. So powerful and timely was this hybrid that to this day it continues to thrive and evolve.[18]

Separating from the Mother

Klein, Fairbairn, and Spitz, each in their own way, subtly shifted the clinical focus from the role of the father to the role of the mother in psychic development. Twenty-five years earlier, Jung had initiated a similar reorientation in his seminal text, *Psychology of the Unconscious*, especially in the chapters entitled "The Battle for Deliverance from the Mother" and "The Dual Mother." The shift in clinical emphasis from the father to the mother in psychic development had played a pivotal role in his theoretical conflict with Freud.[19] Jung began his career as a supporter of Freud, only to come into conflict with him later over

---

[17] Grosskurth, p. 320.

[18] Michael Fordham, *Freud, Jung, Klein—The Fenceless Field: Essays on Psychoanalysis and Analytical Psychology*, ed. R. Hobdell (London: Routledge, 1995). See also, Michael Adams, *The Fantasy Principle: Psychoanalysis of the Imagination* (Hove, UK: Routledge, 2004), pp. 40-49 for a cogent discussion of the similarities and differences between Jung and Fairbairn, especially with respect to Jung's use of the word 'image' in relation to Fairbairn's "internal object" and "endopsychic structure." While Fairbairn denies these terms are equivalent to ego psychology's *representations* or Jungian *imagoes*, his actual *use* of the terms, at times, appears to be remarkably similar. Where Fairbairn differs significantly from both Klein and Jung is in his view of 'internal objects' as compensatory substitutes for actual persons in the outer world, not as essential accompaniments of all experience (Klein) nor as imagoes integrating inner and outer reality (Jung). His understanding of psychic compensation is, however, similar to Jung's. See W. Ronald D. Fairbairn, *An Object-Relations Theory of Personality* (New York: Basic Books, 1954), for a detailed discussion of Fairbairn's term 'internal object.' See also, Judith M. Hughes, *Reshaping the Psychoanalytic Domain: The Works of Melanie Klein, W. R. D. Fairbairn & D. W. Winnicott* (Berkeley, CA: University of California Press, 1989), pp. 89-126.

[19] C. G. Jung, *Psychology of the Unconscious: A Study of the Transformations and Symbolism of the Libido*, tr. B. M. Hinkle, orig. Ger. ed. (1912), Bollingen Series XX (Princeton: Princeton University Press, 1991).

theoretical differences with respect to the primacy of sexuality over psychic images and the role of the mother in psychic development. The conflict with Jung was only the latest in a series of broken male friendships Freud experienced, beginning in the 1890s with Fliess and Breuer, followed by Adler in 1911, and Jung, Ferenzi, and Rank shortly thereafter. As with Fliess and Breuer, Jung's separation from Freud following the publication of *Psychology of the Unconscious* was part political drama, part theoretical difference.

Jung differed with Freud over many theoretical issues that have since found their way back into mainstream psychoanalysis through object relations theory: the importance of the mother in psychic life, the role of mutuality in analysis, the regressive *and* progressive aspects of symptoms, the concept of the self (as opposed to ego), the deliteralization of sexuality, and the constructive use of the analyst's personality in the therapeutic process. Jung opened up clinical pathways later explored through relational psychology and intersubjectivity, especially regarding the early emotional attunement between mother and child and how this dynamic is later played out in analysis.[20] Jung believed that an analyst who meets the emotional needs of the client, like the mother who attends emotionally to the fussy baby instead of just letting it cry, is more likely to have a transformative effect on the emotional state of the analysand.[21]

Bridging Classical Psychoanalysis and Object Relations Theory

In the 1950s and 60s, two analysts, Margaret Mahler and Edith Jacobson, played major roles in attempting to bridge the gulf between classical psychoanalysis (and id psychology) and the new object relations theory. Margaret Mahler was a child analyst and pediatrician who trained in Vienna before moving to New York City. She extended the framework of Spitz's theory to the study of childhood psychosis. While psychoanalysis had struggled with the treatment of neurosis since its inception, psychosis had, for the most part, been beyond the bounds of

---

[20] Jung, *The Psychology of the Transference*, CW 16 § 353-539.

[21] In the past, Jung's contributions have been minimized by many Freudians for political as well as theoretical reasons. As a more balanced and objective assessment of the marginalized dissidents of psychoanalysis begins to take place, Jung's rightful position in the history of psychoanalysis is increasingly being established. See Sonu Shamdasani, *Jung and the Making of Modern Psychology: The Dream of a Science* (Cambridge: Cambridge University Press, 2003), for a comprehensive account of the impact of Jung's work on the social and intellectual history of the twentieth century.

psychoanalytic treatment. Jung, Paul Federn, and some of the followers of Klein had attempted to treat severely disturbed patients, but they were outside of mainstream psychoanalysis. Freud originally conceived of libido as object-oriented, bonding the child to the outer world. When he later attempted to expand his theory to include psychosis, Freud formulated a new concept of primary narcissism in which the initial form of libido is directed towards the inner world. Freud's new theory of libido defined psychosis as a mental condition in which the libido had detached from external objects and withdrawn back into a state of pathological self-absorption.[22]

Mahler extended Spitz's emphasis on the crucial role of early self-other relationships, initiating a more constructive exploration of severe disturbances in childhood. Freud's view of psychosis as a state of primary narcissism Mahler reconceptualized as a disturbance in the formation of the self. Psychosis is not acute self-absorption, but a profound disturbance in the boundary between self and other. Through a careful study of both normal and disturbed children, Mahler reformulated the psychoanalytic understanding of the early stages of primary narcissism, which Freud had previously characterized as objectless. By breaking down the child's developmental journey through successive states of psychic organization, birth to nine months, nine to fifteen months, and fifteen to twenty-four months, Mahler carefully documented the evolving interplay between the child's physical, cognitive, and psychological development, especially with an eye towards the critical function performed by the mother in the infant's evolving sense of self.[23]

Mahler's studies revealed that severe developmental disturbances occurring between the primary caregiver and the infant during the first three years of life often result in pre-Oedipal pathology. Whereas neurosis manifests itself as conflictual indecision, guilt, or discrete symptoms, pre-Oedipal psychopathology appears more as a global disturbance of psychological functioning—for example, extreme disturbances in the boundary between self and other; inability to establish long-term emotional relationships; acute, unregulated feeling states; extreme

---

[22] For a discussion of Freud's case of the psychotic Dr. Schreber from a Jungian perspective, see Michael Adams, *Fantasy Principle*, pp. 76-130.

[23] Margaret S. Mahler, *The Selected Papers of Margaret S. Mahler, Vol. I: Infantile Psychosis and Early Contributions* (New York: Jason Aronson, 1979), pp. 109-192; Gerald Schoenewolf, *Turning Points in Analytic Therapy: From Winnicott to Kernberg* (Northvale, NJ: Jason Aronson, 1990), pp. 79-98.

disturbances in images of self and other; self-mutilation; and severe depression. Mahler's work enabled clinicians to provide better treatment for children and adults suffering from early developmental disturbances. However, the clinical and theoretical contributions of both Spitz and Mahler had relevance far beyond their application to psychopathology. Where Freud had conceived of the 'baby' as an infant filled with untamed instinctual tensions brought partially under control through socialization by the superego, Mahler and Spitz re-imagined the 'baby' as beginning in a symbiotic state with the mother and emerging through a series of stages as an independent autonomous individual: psychological birth is a gradual developmental process, not coincident with emergence from the womb.[24]

Differentiating Self from Other Images

The second significant figure responsible for bridging classical psychoanalysis and object relations is Edith Jacobson (1897-1978). Originally a member of the Berlin Psychoanalytic Society, Jacobson fled Germany for New York City in 1938. Proposing that biology and experience influence each other throughout development, Jacobson worked to bridge Freud's emphasis on constitutional factors, the drives, and the new developmental emphasis on the role of the environment. By focusing her clinical inquiry on the role psychic images play in the formation of mental structure and psychopathology, Jacobson significantly revised Freud's metapsychology.[25] *The infant's earliest subjectively felt experiences are represented as self images and object images.* When the baby feels good, images of a positive, loving mother and a happy, content self build up in the child's psyche. When the baby experiences frustrating or aggressive feelings, images of an unloving mother and an angry, frustrated self accrue. Jacobson theorized that the infant's deepest subjective sense of self and other is an outgrowth of these early images, which provide the infant with a set of lenses through which subsequent experience is continually filtered and organized. The *infant's ability to differentiate images of self from images of others* begins to take place at approximately six to eighteen months of age and is essential for

---

[24] Margaret S. Mahler, Fred Pine, & Anni Bergman, *The Psychological Birth of the Human Infant* (New York: Basic Books, 1975), pp. 39-122.

[25] Edith Jacobson, *The Self and the Object World* (New York: International Universities Press, 1964).

the emergence of a cohesive sense of self as an autonomous entity distinct from the mother/other.[26]

Affectively Integrated Images

A second task confronting the infant during this critical six- to eighteen-month period is the development of the ability to image the mother as a discrete presence who is *both loving and frustrating*. The development of the infant's ability to integrate gratifying and angry aspects of self and other images lays the groundwork for the child to manage conflictual-feeling states later in life. Through this normal developmental process the extreme emotions of love and hate are replaced with more subtle feeling states. The child becomes emotionally able to be hurt or disappointed by someone but still love that person. The *development of affectively integrated images* in the child allows for more complicated emotional experiences and the ability to tolerate differences interpersonally between one's feeling state and that of a significant other.[27]

Edith Jacobson's work on the role played by psychic images in the early relationship between self and object world has made a profound contribution to depth psychology, constructing important conceptual bridges between classical psychoanalysis and object relations theory.[28]

Borderline Personality Disorder

Although orthodox psychoanalysis included an emphasis on ego psychology after Freud's death, it did not admit object relations theory to its inner circle until the late 1960s and early 70s. The two figures most responsible for bringing object relations theory to the United States, and then to center stage in the International Psychoanalytic Association, were Otto Kernberg and Heinz Kohut.

---

[26] This phase is marked by the infant's ability to recognize its own image in a mirror and has been called by Lacan the mirror stage. Failure to develop the capacity to differentiate self from object images may lead to infantile psychosis. See Edith Jacobson, *Psychotic Conflict and Reality* (New York: International Universities Press, 1967).

[27] Edith Jacobson, "On the Psychoanalytic Theory of Affects," *Depression: Comparative Studies of Normal, Neurotic, and Psychotic Conditions* (New York: International Universities Press, 1971), pp. 3-41; Schoenewolf, *Turning Points in Analytic Therapy*, pp. 99-116.

[28] Pine, pp. 206-244; Mitchell & Black, pp. 48-57.

In the late 1960s, Kernberg began to publish a series of clinical papers on character pathology which carefully differentiated borderline personality disorder from neurotic and psychotic conditions.[29] Shifting the diagnostic focus away from neurotic symptoms to the structural determinants of character, *Kernberg analyzed disturbances of internal object relations.* Drawing on Jacobson's earlier work, Kernberg described the development of the infant's ego as involving two essential tasks. First, the infant must develop the capacity to clarify the distinction between self and other. Failure to develop the ability to distinguish self from object images opens the infant to the possibility of delusions, hallucinations, depersonalization, and psychic fragmentation. These psychotic symptoms all reflect disturbances in the ability to differentiate self and object images.[30]

The second task encountered in the development of the infant's ego is the integration of erotically and aggressively toned images. Even though the infant is, after the first phase, able to differentiate self from object images, the images still remain *affectively segregated.* Kernberg theorized that positive self and object images are held together by erotic-libidinal affects. On the other hand, negative self and object images are joined by aggressive affects. This normal emotional segregation is overcome as the infant develops the ability to experience whole objects. *A 'whole object' is an image that integrates both positive and negative, gratifying and frustrating, dimensions of the infant's emotional experience.* If the child develops the capacity to differentiate self from object images, but fails to integrate the positive and negative aspects of self and object images, the result may be a *borderline personality organization.*[31]

Kernberg's clinical explanation of the developmental failure leading to a borderline personality organization folds object relations theory back into the more traditional theory of drives and id psychology. For Kernberg, *failure to integrate the positive and negative aspects of the image results from a pathological excess of "primitive oral*

---

[29] Otto Kernberg, "A Psychoanalytic Classification of Character Pathology," *Journal of the American Psychoanalytic Association* 18 (1971): 800-802; Otto Kernberg, "New Developments in Psychoanalytic Object Relations Theory. Parts I and III Normal and Pathological Development." Presented to the American Psychoanalytic Association, Washington, D. C., 1971 (Unpublished).

[30] Otto Kernberg, *Borderline Conditions and Pathological Narcissism* (New York: Jason Aronson, 1975), pp. 162-166.

[31] Otto Kernberg, "Early Ego Integration and Object Relations," *Annals of the New York Academy of Sciences* 193 (1972): 233-247.

aggression."[32] The inability to integrate the positive and negative affects produces disturbances in the following areas: (1) object constancy; (2) object relations; and (3) self-concept. Whereas repression is the major defense mechanism found in neurosis, Kernberg observed that splitting predominates in pre-Oedipal psychopathology. Splitting is the primary defense used to separate the positive from the negative aspects of self and object images.

Through his integration of id psychology with object relations theory, Kernberg brought his contributions to the study of narcissistic and borderline disorders into alignment with mainstream psychoanalytic theory. His descriptions of self and object representations is in line with the more traditional formulations of Jacobson, the theories of Mahler, Hartmann, and Rappaport, and the techniques of Stone and Lowenstein. Through the use of object relations theory, Kernberg was able to shed new light on the diagnostic obscurities and treatment impasses of pre-Oedipal psychopathology, especially through his formulation of the structural derivatives of object relations. Psychoanalysis as a theory was expanded to include more than just psychopathology originating from intrapsychic conflict. Kernberg's theoretical formulations opened up the possibility of treating severe characterological, narcissistic, borderline, and psychotic disorders and have brought into focus *the central role played by psychic images, the "representational world," both in the ontogenesis of pre-Oedipal pathology and the normal process of psychic structuralization.*[33]

Kernberg's clinical observations and theoretical formulations brought together descriptive approaches, developmental research, and clinical studies, culminating in the inclusion of the diagnostic category 'borderline personality disorder' in the *DSM–III, Diagnostic and Statistical Manual of the American Psychiatric Association.*

Psychology of the Self

Object relations theory and the study of narcissistic personality disorders came together again in the United States in the late 1960s and 1970s through the work of Heinz Kohut, especially in his analysis of

---

[32] Otto Kernberg, *Aggression in Personality Disorders and Perversions* (New Haven, CT: Yale University Press, 1992), pp. 119-140.
[33] Schoenewolf, pp. 197-216; Mitchell & Black, pp. 174-180.

the pathologies of the self.[34] While Kohut initially presented his ideas within existing psychoanalytic theory, he later replaced traditional structural and metapsychological theory with his new "psychology of the self." While Kernberg emphasized the role of aggression and primitive defenses, Kohut, following Spitz and Jacobson, shifted his focus to the external world, especially to the mother's availability and attunement to the infant's phase-appropriate needs. The central difference between Kernberg and Kohut revolves around whether narcissistic and borderline pathology results from defenses against intrapsychic conflict (i.e. splitting) or developmental arrest (repeated empathic failures on the part of the primary caregiver).

To understand better the difference between Kernberg and Kohut, let us take a closer look at this problem from a developmental perspective. The infant achieves the ability to evoke the image of the mother in her absence around six to eighteen months of age. During this time, the development of the child's capacity to evoke the mother's image and her associated empathic holding actions, enables the infant to manage psychically—'to contain'—the anxiety and sense of aloneness resulting from separation. From Kohut's perspective, if there are significant deficits in positive soothing introjects during this period resulting from inadequate maternal holding experiences, borderline and narcissistic pathology may result. Kohut concluded that the adult borderline patient has intense reactions to separation on account of *deficits on the representational level.*

In responding to Kernberg's position that the etiologically significant event is splitting based on excessive oral aggression, rather than a representational deficit, later self psychologists, notably Gerald Adler and Dan Buie, pointed out that this primary inner representational deficit is present from the beginning in the borderline's psyche; consequently, there is no good object representation to be separated from the bad representation through the defense mechanism of splitting.[35] This is an important and persuasive clinical argument.

Kohut's new theory of self psychology developed out of his work with extremely sensitive patients suffering from narcissistic personality disorders and acute problems of self-esteem regulation. Traditionally, this

---

[34] Heinz Kohut, *The Analysis of the Self: A Systematic Approach to the Psychoanalytic Treatment of Narcissistic Personality Disorder* (New York: International University Press, 1971); Heinz Kohut, *The Restoration of the Self* (New York: International Universities Press, 1977).

[35] Gerald Adler & Dan H. Buie, "Aloneness and Borderline Psychopathology: Developmental Issues," *International Journal of Psychoanalysis* 60 (1979): 83-96.

population had been excluded from psychoanalytic treatment based on the theoretical belief that they are incapable of establishing a transference neurosis, and therefore not amenable to psychoanalytic treatment. Kohut discovered transferences in these patients, although different from those encountered in patients suffering from classical neuroses. The new transference configurations Kohut discovered reflect specific selfobject needs being experienced by the patient in the therapeutic relationship. The three dominant forms of transference found in these patients are the *mirror*, *idealizing*, and *twinship*. Each form of transference is determined by particular deficits in the patient's self development. These transferences are fundamentally different from those encountered in patients with a cohesive self structure. The earlier developmental needs for mirroring and/or idealizing, which were not fulfilled in childhood, are reactivated in the transference in an attempt to restore the cohesiveness and vitality of the patient's self representation. Kohut's new *self psychology* replaces the primacy of drives in psychoanalytic theory with the primacy of selfobject experiences.[36]

Psychoanalytic theory in the 1970s was significantly altered by Kernberg's and Kohut's shift in clinical focus to the role of object relations and selfobject experiences in pre-Oedipal psychopathology. The 1970s were marked by another significant shift in clinical and theoretical focus, this time by one that called into question the very foundation of depth psychology. While psychoanalysis was based clinically on the 'talking cure,' it was grounded theoretically on a biological and economic model: the theory of drives and libido. This situation changed dramatically during the 1970s, first through Kohut's replacement of drives with selfobject functions, followed by movements from various quarters *to establish linguistics, rather than biology, as the foundation and model for psychoanalysis*. Marshall Edelson replaced the economic model with generative grammar;[37] Roy Schafer substituted "action language" for Freud's metapsychology;[38] and Jacques Lacan

---

[36] Lionel Corbett & Paul Kugler, "The Self in Jung and Kohut," *Dimensions of Self Experience*, ed. A. Goldberg (Hillsdale, NJ: The Analytic Press, 1989).

[37] Marshall Edelson, *Language and Interpretation in Psychoanalysis* (New Haven, CT: Yale University Press, 1975).

[38] Roy Schafer, *A New Language for Psychoanalysis* (New Haven, CT: Yale University Press, 1976).

exchanged the biological foundation for a foundation in structural linguistics.[39]

Deliteralization of Theory

Attention to theoretical foundations shifted again in the 1980s, this time to a questioning of the very notion of theory itself. Perhaps nothing is more characteristic of depth psychology in the 1980s and 90s than the movement towards deliteralization of theory. The traditional notion of theory as a concrete explanation of original facts was being replaced by the notion of theory as a constructive narrative; consequently, the view of personality as originating in literal events began to give way to the view that *personality is self-reflexively constructed through narrative*. This theoretical shift has become pervasive in psychoanalysis. This focus on the constructive, fictional dimension of personality inevitably led to the question of the origin of a self capable of self-reflection. The question of what constitutes subjectivity and its characteristic reflexivity is the central question in all of depth psychology. How does a self become capable of looking back at itself and, thereby, develop the capacity to differentiate unconscious from conscious, literal from metaphoric, object from subject? Under what conditions is human reflexivity defined? Under what conditions is it reversed?[40]

The 'Origin' of Self-Reflection

The question of how a self becomes self-conscious led inevitably in a reflexive way to the further question of *how the construction of human personality occurs in and through the various symbol systems available in any given space and time*. The question of the origin of self-consciousness itself has become so strangely reflexive that the theories in which we talk about the construction of personality have themselves become self-consciously constructed. We have begun to see the fictionality of the very theories through which we construct our "myths of human personality."[41]

---

[39] Jacques Lacan, *Ecrits,* tr. A. Sheridan (New York: W. W. Norton & Co., 1977); Jacques Lacan, *The Four Fundamental Concepts of Psychoanalysis*, tr. A. Sheridan (New York: W. W. Norton & Co., 1978)s.

[40] Paul Kugler, "Jacques Lacan: Post-Modern Depth Psychology and the Birth of the Self-Reflexive Subject," *The Book of the Self: Person, Pretext, and Process*, eds. P. Eisendrath & J. Hall (New York: New York University Press, 1987).

[41] James Hillman, *The Myth of Analysis* (Evanston, IL: Northwestern University Press, 1972).

This realization came about in England and the United States partly through systematic and empirical work with mothers and infants. In other countries, it occurred by other means. In France, among the Lacanians, for example, the same issue was raised, not through empirical data, but in much more theoretical terms and through philosophical lenses. But the issue remains the same: How can we understand human subjectivity so as to account for both the presence and the absence of reflexivity in human beings? How can we define the human subject so as to account for both its reflexive possibility and the possibility of its loss?

The human subject with its characteristic reflexivity cannot come into being without the participation of an elaborate symbolic universe. Without the capacity for a self to represent itself, either as an image or as a word, and thereby look back at itself from another perspective, the construction of personality and its characteristic capacity for memory and self-reflection, would be impossible. *A self capable of self-reflection does not come into being without the participation of an elaborate linguistic and/or representational universe; this cultural matrix must be present from the beginning, analogous to the cultural base in which bacteria originate.*

The Mirror Stage

The soul cannot exist without its other side, which is always found in a "you."[42]
—C. G. Jung

Throughout the history of depth psychology, there has been the assumption that human personality is characterized by an inherently divided, double kind of psychic reality. It is 'divided' in that all psychic conflict has to do with experiencing the personality as divided, whether into consciousness and unconsciousness, or into various complexes, or into a more elaborate 'ego, id, and super-ego' structure. In its 'double' aspect, it is divided in a very different sense: 'double' implies capable of, and, in a sense, doomed to, a kind of self-reflection. So, how does this 'divided subject' doomed to self-reflection come into being?

---

[42] Jung, *CW* 16 § 545.

The development of the capacity for self-reflection in the child has been described by Lacan as the mirror stage. The story of the birth of self-reflexivity begins early in life. The scene is set in the home, and the principle actor is an infant, six months to a year in age, not yet able to talk. All at once, the child, who has never before hesitated in passing before a mirror, stops and smiles, for this is the first time the infant recognizes itself in a mirror. *The development of the child's capacity to identify with its own image in a mirroring relationship is the action upon which all subjectivity is based.* It is the moment human reflexivity is born. The infant's discovery of and identification with its 'own image' differentiates the personality into conscious and unconscious, representational ego and experiential self. *The constitution of a psychic sense of otherness results from the realization that the reflected representation actually 'belongs' to the same child viewing and experiencing the psychic image as other.* Octavio Paz describes the subject's experience of otherness this way:

> "Otherness" is above all the simultaneous perception that we are others without ceasing to be what we are and that, without ceasing to be where we are, our true being is in another place.[43]

As the infant *views its own image as other* in a mirroring relationship, the very act of viewing simultaneously brings into being the 'subjectivity' of the viewer. During the mirror stage the infant's psyche develops the capacity to imagine itself and reflect on its own self-representation. The act of self-reflection is the specular experience of the psychic image and the infant's biological experience separated only by the amount of time it takes the reflected light to return to the child's eye. The act of reflection mixes up the two heterogeneous 'subjects,' the image and the biological, the other and the self, the fictional and the autobiographical, at a speed no less than the speed of light.

---

[43] Octavio Paz, *The Bow and the Lyre*, tr. R. Simms (New York: McGraw-Hill, 1975), p. 245.

Psychic Image and Bodily Experience

The mirror would do well to reflect a little more before returning our image to us.[44]
—Jacques Lacan

This infinitely fast oscillation between these two heterogeneous subjects constitutes the birth of the divided psyche and its inherent reflexivity. The extraordinary economy of such an allegorical event, a child looking in a mirror, perfectly normal in its drama and staging, spontaneously deconstructs the oppositional logic that lies in the Western categorical distinctions between image and 'the real.' The 'first act' of self-reflection in a mirroring relationship produces the very drama it re-views. It is the play and the re-play, the action and the re-action, the cognition and the re-cognition in an infinitely fast oscillation contained within a single event. The child's dramatic performance of the mirror stage consists simply in producing 'its self.' *It is a reflection that creates the self of self-reflection by creating the drama in the very act of re-viewing it.*

While other animals, such as apes, cats, and dogs, are capable of perceiving the image of their body in the mirror, only the human infant develops the ability to grasp the reciprocal relation between self and its reflection. This sets the stage for language acquisition and the development of symbolic thought.

In "Mirror-Role of Mother and Family in Child Development," Winnicott adopts an analogous view of the constitution of selfhood: "[E]ach child derives benefit from being able to see himself or herself in the attitude of the individual members or in the attitudes of the family as a whole." A real mirror is not a prerequisite for development of the maturational process of mirroring for either Winnicott or Lacan: "The actual mirror has significance mainly in its figurative sense."[45]

The mirror stage is a paradigmatic metaphor for the birth of self-reflective consciousness and the mutual dependence between these two heterogeneous subjects. There can be no reflection without the biological child and there can be no consciousness of the biological

---

[44] Lacan, *Ecrits,* p. 138.
[45] Donald W. Winnicott, "Mirror-Role of Mother and Family in Child Development," *Playing and Reality* (Harmondsworth, UK: Penguin Books, 1971), p. 138.

child without the child's image. The 'real' and the 'psychic image' are coterminus: each co-implicates the other. Prior to the mirror stage, the child lacks the capacity to distinguish the objective from the subjective. If there is hunger, it is not the child's hunger, for the infant is incapable of conceiving a 'self' separate from the desire. But during the mirror stage, this unity of experience is split and the child develops the capacity to recognize its 'self' in the mirror image.

The differentiation between the actual infant and the image with which the infant identifies is only the anticipation of a far more profound differentiation of the psyche that will occur during language acquisition. The later process of acquiring language replaces the mirror image of the body with a linguistic image, the first-person-singular pronoun: "I" in English. With the acquisition of language comes the ontological rupture that lies between word and experience, between description and event. Through the acquisition of language, the child is ushered into an elaborate linguistic universe, a collective matrix of phonetic symbols. The importance of this linguistic entry into a system of representations cannot be overemphasized. For in acquiring linguistic competence, the infant learns to speak to the world through a network of collectively determined phonetic images.

Constructing the Human Subject

Through the acquisition of language the child is separated from the material world and ushered into a system of phonetic patterns capable of replacing the actual objects of reference. This process lays the foundation for symbolic thought and the development of the human subject. The realization that human subjectivity with its characteristic reflexivity is constructed through metaphorizing leads to the awareness that we are constantly creating metaphors of ourselves, as well as of our understanding of ourselves. Self-consciousness, as well as our myths of self-consciousness, is not a given. Self-consciousness is something constructed in every dimension of our existence, including speaking, imagining, theory making, free-associating, and every other dimension of activity that occurs after the mirror stage and the advent of language. Whether this constructing and metaphorizing activity exists before the psyche is structured through language is impossible to say, but it is certainly an indisputable fact once we begin to inhabit the world of language.[46]

---

[46] For an extended discussion of the relation between psychic images and phonetics, see Paul Kugler, *The Alchemy of Discourse: Image, Sound and Psyche*, rev. ed. (Zürich: Daimon Verlag, 2002).

CHAPTER FOUR

The Jungian Subject

The ego stands to the self as the moved to the mover, or as object to subject, because the determining factors which radiate out from the self surround the ego and are therefore supraordinate to it. ... It is not I who creates myself, rather I happen to myself.[1] — C. G. Jung

Birth of the Subject

In depth psychology we encounter the paradox that the observer is the observed. The psyche is not only the object, but also the subject of the discipline. Our reflexive ability to study the human subject emerged in the seventeenth century through the process of Descartes's *cogito* constituting itself as an object of knowledge.[2] The historical appearance of the notion of the self-reflexive subject characterizes the movement from Medieval Scholasticism to modernity. Prior to Descartes, existence was predicated on a transcendent God, Matter, or Eternal Forms. But with Descartes's *cogito ergo sum*—"I think therefore I am"—the human subject for the first time is placed directly at the center of Western metaphysics and psychological understanding. Descartes's theory of the thinking subject signaled a major change in Western psychological thought, locating the source of meaning, certainty, truth, and existence *within human subjectivity*. The Cartesian *cogito* contains the beginnings of the modern philosophical project to provide an anthropological foundation for our psychology and metaphysics. No longer are ideal forms (Plato), matter (Aristotle) or god (medieval philosophy) at the center of our system of thought. Now, at the center, Descartes locates the human subject. But, in the 21st century, we find ourselves once again at a critical moment in the history of

---

[1] C. G. Jung, *The Collected Works of C. G. Jung*, tr. R. F. C. Hull, vol. 11 (Princeton: Princeton University Press, 1971), para. 391. All subsequent references to Jung's *Collected Works*, abbreviated to *CW*, will be by volume and paragraph number, designated by §.

[2] Michel Foucault, *The Order of Things: An Archaeology of the Human Sciences* (New York: Random House, 1970).

Western psychology. Today we are witnessing a transformation in our underlying system of thought that is every bit as dramatic as the movement in the 17th century out of scholastic and medieval assumptions about human nature.

Death of the Subject

Nietzsche's declaration of the Death of God in the last quarter of the 19th century signaled the beginning of the end of modernity. Through a radical questioning of the transcendent values that Scholasticism and Modernism had assumed as givens, Nietzsche attempted to call forth a transvaluation of values and the birth of a new conception of the human subject. In recent years, the foundations of modernity are once again being challenged. This time the challenge is being heralded by Roland Barthes' and Michel Foucault's declaration of the 'death of the subject.' The existence of the very 'subject' that declared god dead one hundred years ago is now being called into question. *Speaking subjects* are no longer assumed to be the unquestionable source of language and speech, existence and truth, unity and wholeness, identity and individuality. The transcendence of Descartes's *cogito* is no longer so certain.

Each time the first-person-singular pronoun is uttered, the 'I' projects a different agency, a different perspective and identity. The speaking subject appears not to be a single referent beyond the first-person-singular pronoun, but rather a pluralistic entity produced by the act of speaking. The representational ego, the 'I,' is a function of its place within a larger network of linguistic structures. The 'I' is to language what the ego is to the (Jungian) self.

Subject and its Relation to Language

Human subjectivity comes into being not beyond language, but in and through it. The 'I' is a function of the place, the position, the site it holds within the textual realm. Language might be compared to a game of chess. The significance of each piece is determined by its place in relation to all the other pieces, not by its material substance. In like manner, a word's location within a particular discourse determines its significance. For example, the meaning of the first-person-singular pronoun, 'I', is uniquely determined each time it is located in a particular text.

This ontological shift from the primacy of the individual subject to the text has produced a Copernican revolution. It is not simply a change in perspective, but an entirely new mode of thought, a different way of conceiving the world and its relation to the human psyche. Historically, the 'certainties' in our systems of thought have been founded on the belief in god or the gods, common sense, empirical observation, or phenomenological experience. But with the emerging recognition of *the irreducibly textual character of our beliefs and our theories*, traditional ontological foundations are being challenged. As our certainty in theoretical foundations is called into question, so too is our understanding of psychological concepts. Concepts such as 'I,' 'subject,' 'self,' 'reality,' 'dream,' 'unconscious,' and 'psyche' are, after all, words within the larger system of language and cannot be regarded as transparent to either their meaning or referent. A careful analysis of the relation between human subjectivity and language reveals that all psychological theory is trapped within the confines of language, unable to stray beyond the limits of its own terms. Once language is acquired and the first-person-singular pronoun, 'I,' enters into an individual's linguistic system of symbols, escape from the conceptual web embedding psychological concepts is impossible. We simply cannot step outside of language and speak about it from some other perspective. While depth psychology has been aware of this epistemological limitation with respect to the psyche for nearly a century, only recently has this limitation been recognized with respect to language as well.[3]

Imago and Psychic Text

To gain a better understanding of this ontological shift and its implications for depth psychology, let us turn for a moment to Jung's notion of the 'imago' and see if its *representational qualities* bear any family resemblance to the contemporary notion of 'text.' How is the term 'imago' defined? What is the imago's relation to its referent and meaning? And how is the imago related to dream interpretation?

---

[3] Jacques Derrida, *Of Grammatology*, tr. G. C. Spivak (Baltimore: The Johns Hopkins University Press, 1974). Derrida boldly states that we "cannot legitimately transgress the text toward something other than it, toward a referent (a reality that is metaphysical, historical, psychobiographical, etc.) .... There is nothing outside the text" (p. 158).

The imago is a living image composed of outer perceptions and inner apperceptions. Sense impressions from the external world entering via the perceptual systems are transfigured by emotional reactions creating an imago which *reflects* the external world with considerable qualifications. The imago is not simply a *reproduction* of the outer world (i.e. a copy of a historical event) or of the physiological world (i.e. a representation of a drive), but a psychic *production*.[4]

In Jungian psychology, the realm of psychic images is referred to as the *imaginal*, while in the Freudian tradition, this realm has come to be called the *imaginary*. Rarely is the distinction between the two terms discussed in professional literature, and yet, it carries considerable theoretical and clinical significance. The difference between the imaginal and the imaginary has a long and complicated history in philosophy, reflecting the uncertainty in Western metaphysics regarding the ontological status of psychic images. Freudian theory has traditionally assumed a reproductive view of images. For example, id psychology viewed psychic images as *representations of drives* and Lacan later reconceived of them as representations of 'the real.' The imago's inability to portray, represent, accurately some purportedly more primary reality, e.g., the drive, the body or the 'real,' has led Lacanians, in particular, to *distrust the imaginary*. From this perspective, 'failure' of the psychic image to perform its purported reproductive function, results in 'misunderstanding' and a hermeneutics of suspicion.

In Jungian psychology, on the other hand, the function of imagoes is not to represent some other, purportedly more primary reality, but rather, to *create our conscious experience of psychic reality*. In describing this process, Jung writes: "The psyche creates reality every day. The only expression I can use for this activity is *fantasy*. ... Fantasy, therefore, seems to me the clearest expression of the specific activity of the psyche. It is, pre-eminently ... a creative activity."[5]

The Jungian Self: A Subject Superordinate to the Ego

Jung's most important contribution to the history of the subject in Western thought is his realization, as early as the 1920s, that within the personality there is not one, but two subjects. At the time, this was

---

[4] Jung, *CW* 16 § 305.
[5] Jung, *CW* 6 § 78.

a radically new idea. Jung conceived of the ego as the conscious subject and formulated the idea of a second, more primary psychological structure which includes the conscious *and* unconscious dimensions of the psyche. This superordinate other subject, Jung called the self. The ego in its relation to the self holds a position similar to the role of the subject in relation to discourse in critical theory. As the Cartesian subject has lost its primary ontological status to language, so too has the ego lost its primacy to the self.

The self is conceptualized as the agency within the psyche, superordinate to the ego, moving the personality towards maturity and completion. Striving towards representing the totality of the psyche, it functions as a self-regulating agency, an internal self-care system. While conceiving of the self as the agency in the personality responsible for psychic cohesion, the creation of personal values, self-esteem, and individuation, Jung also acknowledged that the self concept is a theoretical fiction: "So far, I have found no stable or definite center in the unconscious and I don't believe such a center exists. I believe that the thing which I call the Self is an ideal center ... that dream of totality."[6] Jung's concept of the self lies somewhere between the modernist notion of the subject and the post-modern notion of discourse or perhaps Heidegger's being of language. While Jung's original notion of the self differs from that of the modernist 'subject,' it still carries certain of the modernist characteristics: a privileged status, a totalizing tendency, and the sense of a unitary, singular identity.

Freudian Reformulations of the Self

Let us turn for a moment to Lacan's divided subject, its origin and structure. For the notion of the post-mirror-stage 'divided subject' Lacan is indebted to earlier work by Wallon and Hegel. A French psychologist of the 1930s, Henri Wallon conducted experiments with young children using mirrors to study the origin of self-reflectivity. The literal mirror

---

[6] Quoted in Miguel Serrano, *C. G. Jung and Hermann Hesse: A Record of Two Friendships*, tr. F. MacShane (New York: Schocken Books, 1968), p. 50. When writing about the self, Jung acknowledges, at least on a theoretical level, that the self-as-such is ultimately unknowable: "I trust I have given no cause for the misunderstanding that I know anything about the nature of the 'center' [the self]—for it is simply unknowable ...." (Jung, *CW* 12 § 327). When referring to the self as the totality of the psyche in distinction from the ego, many Jungians have adopted the convention of capitalizing the 's' in self.

Wallon used with his experimental subjects Lacan later transformed into a metapsychological concept, a metaphor to explain the genesis of human subjectivity. In addition to drawing on Wallon's work, Lacan adopted a modified version of Hegel's account of the origin of the human subject through the dialectical process of self-alienation and negativity.[7] For Lacan, the genesis of subjectivity resides in the infant's seeing its self-same image in the dialectical encounter with the specular image in the mirror. This differs from Winnicott's view, in which the *empathic reflection in the other need only be 'good enough,'* not self-same. The structure of Lacan's mirror stage, with its need for the infant to see its self-same image, is driven by the logic of the modern flat mirror. The reflection of the flat mirror produces a v*erisimilitude* and limits the process only to the specular image. Are there not, however, many other 'mirrors' empathically reflecting back the child's reality? The mother's arms and legs kinesthetically reflect the presence of the infant. The tactile dimensions of her skin reflect warmth or coolness, loving or stern affective responses. The gleam in the mother's eye reflects important emotional values, while the tone in her voice resonates with a variety of different feeling states. Each one of these 'mirrors' uniquely reflects the child through different reflective structures.[8]

The *difference* between the child's bodily experience and its reflected image in the other may be understood not merely as misleading, but also as essential. There is a natural, healthy difference between the child's experience and the reflections it perceives in the primary caregiver. The reflected 'image' that appears in the face of the (m)other empathically relating to the child is not static, but dynamic, alive, ever changing, reflecting the fluctuations in her emotional attunement to the infant.

---

[7] "The dialectic which supports our experiences ... obliges us to understand the ego as being constituted from top to bottom within the movement of progressive alienation in which self-consciousness is constituted in Hegel's phenomenology." Jacques Lacan, *Ecrits*, tr. A. Sheridan (New York: W. W. Norton & Co., 1977), p. 374. For a Hegelian reading of Jungian psychology see Wolfgang Giegerich, *The Soul's Logical Life: Towards a Rigorous Notion of Psychology* (Frankfurt am Main: Peter Lang, 1998).

[8] In the history of Western culture there has been a succession of different types of mirrors. The modern flat mirror used by Wallon in his experiments and later adopted by Lacan as a metapsychological concept, is only the latest mirror in a long tradition. For a psychological understanding of the role the particular mirror structure plays in psychic life, see David L. Miller, "Through a Looking Glass: The World as Enigma," *Eranos 55-1986* (Frankfurt am Main: Insel Verlag, 1988), pp. 349-402. See also, Sabine Melchior-Bonnet, *The Mirror: A History*, tr. K. H. Jewett (New York: Routledge, 2001); Christine Downing, "Prologue," *Mirrors of the Self* (Los Angeles: J. P. Tarcher Publishing, 1991), pp. ix-xx; and James W. Fernandez, "Reflections on Looking into Mirrors," *Semiotica* 30.1-2 (1980): 27-39.

The specular image in a flat mirror, however, does not possess the living emotional qualities of *empathy and recognition* so necessary for the healthy development of a sense of intersubjectivity and interiority. *The living image being reflected back by another subject, is not self-same, but a combination of sameness and difference. Essential aspects of the child are being reflected back along with the unique emotional response of the other.*[9] This process results in differentiation, self-consciousness, psychic cohesion, and emotional enrichment, as well as in a certain degree of misunderstanding and distress. As the child internalizes the reflected 'image,' a psychic 'weaning' begins to occur, a self-differentiation from a primary unity of experience, resulting in recognition of independent object-forms and the constitution of human subjectivity.[10]

Lacan's theoretical understanding of the onset of subjectivity presents an additional difficulty. According to the logic of the mirror stage, the child has a bodily experience of fragmentation prior to the mirror stage that is in conflict with the apparent wholeness reflected in the specular image. But the *temporal logic* in Lacan's mirror stage is problematic. How can a consciousness of the experience of fragmentation exist prior to the identification with the specular image, if it is precisely the identification with the 'alienated' image that produces the 'knowing subject,' i.e., self-differentiation, recognition, and self-consciousness? *Ontologically, Lacan appears to be inserting a self-knowledge of fragmentation into the as-yet-to-be 'knowing subject,' prior to its constitution.*[11]

Pre-symbolic Self and Verbal Self

The Jungian ego/self structure is not simply a 'divided subject' resulting from the dialectical process of self-alienation during the mirror stage. While the onset of subjectivity and the development of the ego/self dynamic occurs during the mirror stage and the acquisition of language, a rudimentary sense of 'self' appears to begin already at birth.

---

[9] See Daniel Stern, *The Interpersonal World of the Infant* (New York: Basic Books, 1985); Jessica Benjamin, *Shadow of the Other: Intersubjectivity and Gender in Psychoanalysis* (London: Routledge, 1998).

[10] Just as Lacan deliteralized Wallon's mirror, so we, too, need not take the silvering and drama of the theory of the mirror stage too literally.

[11] My own view with respect to the development of the self and the onset of subjectivity is more consistent with Daniel Stern's theory that self development begins much earlier and is already well under way by the time of the constitution of the verbal self.

Daniel Stern's research in early infant observation has led him to theorize that self development begins much earlier than Lacan's mirror stage and is already well under way by the time of language acquisition. Stern differentiates three distinct stages of pre-symbolic self development prior to the constitution of the verbal self: (1) the emergent self (birth to two months); (2) the core self (two to six months); and (3) the subjective self (six to fifteen months). During the first two months, the infant begins to experience "the sense of an emergent self." From the second to the sixth month, the infant begins to form a "core self" characterized by four essential abilities: self-coherence, agency, memory, and self-affectivity. A "subjective self" develops between six and fifteen months through the interactive affective communication between the caregiver and the infant. From fifteen months onward, the infant moves from a pre-symbolic self to a verbal self. Stern's conceptual framework has been adopted by many in the psychoanalytic community for the developmental study of the pre-symbolic human infant. The fourth stage in Stern's developmental model, the verbal self, is analogous to Lacan's mirror stage, which leads to the acquisition of language and the entrance of the infant into a vast symbolic universe.

Jungians and Lacanians have much to learn from each other with respect to the 'divided subject.' Each school of thought has made significant contributions to our understanding of the process of symbolization, the onset of subjectivity, the primacy of the letter in the unconscious,[12] and the structurization of the psyche.

In the 1970s, Kohut's work added significant new insights to our understanding of the development of the self and the structurization of the emotional and ideational life of the child. Through an analysis of the function played by empathic mirroring in the formation of psychic life, Kohut introduced into psychoanalytic theory a revised understanding of the emergence of the self and its pathology. The relationship between ego and self is established through the infant's living relationship with another subject, the primary caregiver, who not only reflects back the infant's self-same presence, but also recognizes the child's existence as other. As this intersubjective dynamic develops, an intrapsychic ego/self structure evolves and the ego experiences the self

---

[12] For an extended analysis of the relation between sound, image and psyche in the work of Jung and Lacan, see Paul Kugler, *The Alchemy of Discourse: Image, Sound and Psyche*, rev. ed. (Zürich: Daimon Verlag, 2002).

as an internal self-care system, promoting psychic containment, engendering self-esteem, and harboring psychic potentials.

Repeated empathic failures on the part of the primary caregiver may result in disturbances to the child's object relations and in the formation of pre-Oedipal psychopathology—psychotic, characterological, narcissistic, or borderline personality disorders. Kohut observed that the functions of the self—holding, containing, and integrating—are originally performed by the primary caregiver, who serves as a selfobject for the child. During the process of maturation, these functions are internalized, forming the core of a healthy self structure in the adult personality. The functions of the self as conceived by Kohut in the 1970s, are similar to the Jungian formulations in the following ways: The self (1) performs a self-regulating function; (2) facilitates integration and a sense of psychic cohesion; (3) contains the potential of self-realization, i.e., is a 'blue print' of the mature personality; (4) promotes a deep sense of personal values; (5) regulates self-esteem; (6) facilitates the development of individual identity; and (7) performs holding and containing functions.[12] From a Jungian perspective, pre-Oedipal psychopathology manifests as a disturbance in the ego's relation to the self. When the ego/self dynamic is significantly damaged through repeated empathic failures on the part of the primary caregiver, the impaired self functions often reappear in the analytic encounter in the transferential forms (mirror, idealized and twinship) described by Kohut.

Objective and Subjective Levels of Dream Interpretation

The naive person takes it as self-evident from the start that when he dreams of Mr. X this dream-image is identical with the real Mr. X. It is an assumption that is entirely in accord with his ordinary, uncritical conscious attitude, which makes no distinction between object as such and the idea one has of it.[13]

—C. G. Jung

Jung developed a therapeutic hermeneutic based upon two levels of interpretation: the objective and the subjective. When approaching a dream on the objective level, the image is referred to the outer world, for example, to an earlier childhood event, a current interpersonal

---

[13] Jung, *CW* 8 § 508.

relationship, or a transference dynamic. This level of interpretation is based on a two-person psychology and uses a reductive analysis to work with the intersubjective aspects of the dream. Images are approached in terms of *unconscious dimensions in the dreamer's relation to the outer world*, whether in current or past interpersonal relationships.

The subjective level of interpretation, on the other hand, shifts the focus to *unconscious subjective dimensions,* referring psychic images to the dreamer's inner world (complexes, ego/self dynamics, and imagoes). Interpretation on the subjective level is based on a one-person psychology and analyzes psychic contents in terms of intrapsychic dynamics, viewing images as relatively autonomous entities making up part of the person's inner world.[14]

Jung's method of dream interpretation is based, in part, on a transformation of Kant's distinction between the noumenal and the phenomenal into a clinical hermeneutic. The objective level approaches the imago as if it were referring to the actual object, the thing-as-such, while the subjective level suspends this assumption, approaching the imago as a psychic phenomenon, a relatively autonomous entity within the personality. On the subjective level, the image is viewed as a primary psychic phenomenon, while on the objective level, the image is viewed in terms of intersubjective dynamics. Clinical interpretation involves a subtle holding of the tension between these two levels of interpretation.[15]

This approach to psychic images unsettles the boundary between subject and object, self and other, subverting at the same time the symmetry that founds their traditional opposition. From the beginning of Greek philosophy, these primordial dualities—inner/outer, mind/body, self/other—have provided the foundation for Western metaphysics. Psychic images have traditionally been located *between* these dualities and they have been assumed to perform a secondary, reproductive function. Kant re-conceived image as performing a

---

[14] Jung, *CW* 7 §121-140.

[15] Jung, *CW* 7. Jung further describes the subjective level of interpretation in *CW* 8 § 509: "The whole dream-work is essentially subjective, and a dream is a theatre in which the dreamer is himself the scene, the player, the promoter, the producer, the author, the public, and the critic. This simple truth forms the basis for a conception of the dream's meaning which I have called *interpretation on the subjective level*. Such an interpretation, as the term implies, conceives all the figures in the dream as personified features of the dreamer's own personality."

primary, originary function, thereby setting the stage for the birth of depth psychology and a radically new understanding of psychic image as performing a productive function and constituting the very essence of being human.

Asymmetrical Mirroring

> *Mirror, mirror on the wall,*
> *Who's the fairest of us all?*
> —Snow White

Perhaps the single most defining characteristic of being human is consciousness and its capacity for reflexivity. Moving between the objective and subjective levels of dream interpretation is a form of self-reflection. It involves the ego reflecting on aspects of the psyche estranged from consciousness. Jung describes the process of dream interpretation in the following passage:

> To concern ourselves with dreams is a way of reflecting on ourselves—a way of self-reflection. It is not our ego-consciousness reflecting on itself; rather, it turns its attention to the objective actuality of the dream.... It reflects not on the ego but on the self; it recollects the strange self, alien to the ego, which was ours from the beginning, the trunk from which the ego grew. It is alien to us because we have estranged ourselves from it through the aberrations of the conscious mind.[16]

Dream analysis involves a form of self-reflection strikingly different from the symmetrical mirroring produced by a flat mirror. Rather than 'mirroring' back the self-same face of ego-consciousness, the dream reflects back the shadowy face of the *other*. The process of self-reflection operating in dream analysis is based more on the logic of mirrors as found in psychic reality than on the logic of those found in physical reality. The images being reflected back in 'our' dreams are not symmetrical to consciousness, but reflect an otherness, foreign to the ego. This model of reflection asymmetrically mirrors back, not the self-same, but its shadow side, the alien other. Through the process of moving from the objective to the subjective level of dream interpretation, alienated

---

[16] Jung, *CW* 10 § 318.

aspects of the psyche are slowly brought into a more integrated relation to consciousness.[17]

The Site of Reflexivity

In *Symbols of Transformation,* Jung discusses the process of interpreting the parental imago with respect to its objective and subjective dimensions. *While experientially a dream takes place within the psyche, it refers to interpersonal as well as to intrapsychic dimensions.*

> Interpretation in terms of the parents is, however, simply a *façon de parler.* In reality the whole drama takes place in the individual's own psyche, where the "parents" are not the parents at all but only their imagoes; they are representations which have arisen from the conjunction of parental peculiarities with the individual disposition of the child.[18]

If we observe carefully what Jung is *performing* in this passage, we find the process of moving from the objective to the subjective level of interpretation is, indeed, simply a manner of speaking (*façon de parler*)! The interpretive move from the objective to the subjective level is accomplished by inserting quotation marks, *transforming the parents into "the parents."* This linguistic act challenges the habitual assumption of referentiality operative in everyday language use, opening up the psychic space between the called and the so-called. *This is the place of quasi-quotation, the topos between the literal and the metaphorical, the site of reflexivity. The imago inhabits the reflexive space between the subject and the object, between the called and the so-called, constructively holding the tension between the literal and the metaphorical without privileging one over the other.*

Lived Experience and the Textual Realm

The differentiation of the actual infant from its psychic representation during the mirror stage is only the anticipation of a far more profound differentiation of the psyche that occurs during language

---

[17] The Jungian hermeneutic based on an intrapsychic and an interpersonal level of interpretation is particularly well suited to work with the various Freudian psychologies: drive theory, ego psychology, object relations, self psychology, and intersubjectivity.

[18] Jung, *CW* 9ii § 505.

acquisition. This latter process replaces the image of the body with a linguistic image, the first-person-singular pronoun. Through the acquisition of language the child is ushered into an elaborate textual universe, a collective matrix of signifiers. This interpersonal realm of symbols is collective and, for the most part, unconscious. The unconscious cannot be limited only to an individual, intrapsychic entity, but is a function of the collectivity which creates and sustains it. The collective unconscious functions as the repository of personal and social myths, as the locus of socially approved images, linguistic signifiers, and narrative structures. Without the notion of a collective symbolic system, an objectively determined code, intersubjective communication through language could not take place. The "I" always comes into being within the context of a collective system of representations, just as selfhood depends on a collectivity of persons to empathically reflect and recognize its emerging identity. Individuation does not lead to individualism, but to a sense that I am not a separate being with my own private and personal experience, but rather, that my selfhood is constituted by others. The development of this sense of 'I'-ness through individuation is not an egoistic (solo) achievement, but a power conferred on the individual by a collective constituency and its objectively determined symbol system—language.

Language and Self/Other Representations

The acquisition of language has three significant effects. In the first place, by acquiring the ability to name itself, the individual is able to symbolize himself or herself by replacing lived experience with a text. This capacity to self-represent allows us to gain consciousness of and distance from the immediacy of an event. The textual realm not only mediates the object world, but also self-experiences by establishing a self-representation in language (e.g. 'I'). For example, this capacity allows a person to recognize his or her ego-image in a lived dream and represent it in a dream text.[19]

---

[19] Paul Kugler, "The Unconscious in a Postmodern Depth Psychology," *C. G. Jung and the Humanities*, ed. K. Barnaby & P. Acierno (Princeton, NJ: Princeton University Press, 1990).

The dialectic between lived experience and the textual realm constitutes an essential part of therapeutic analysis. Since its inception, depth psychology has distinguished itself from other forms of treatment through its commitment to a 'talking cure.' The analysand is placed in a therapeutic relationship in which unconscious dimensions of his or her psyche are encouraged to express themselves on a symbolic level. During the course of analysis, unconscious experiences are 'represented' to consciousness through the particular collective symbol systems available to the individual. Analysis begins with symptoms, dreams, conflicts, and human suffering, and over time, the contents of these experiences are reconstructed by means of words and images, thus creating a framework wherein these psychic experiences can be represented in a symbolic universe.

Every analytic experience occurs within a narrative mode of discourse. For example, the analysand recounts a painful childhood experience, or an enigmatic dream, or speaks of what happened during the previous week, and through decontextualization and recontextualization, a new understanding begins to emerge. The symptom is replaced by discourse, the dream event is replaced by a dream text, an unconscious experience is replaced by a personal narrative. Experiences that had been 'buried' in the body through hysterical conversion or unconsciously projected onto others are relocated into the symbolic 'ground' of narrative structures.

Inner and Outer Texts

The process of analysis works to differentiate the analysand's conscious identity in relation to both the outer and inner texts. The outer texts of a child are those spheres of representation constructed by others in which the child is represented. For example, the outer text might be the parent's discourse: "You have your grandfather's eyes"; "You are mommy's little angel." The child represented in the parent's text is not the same as the actual person. The child literally does not have the grandfather's eyes, nor is the child literally an angel. If the child over-identifies with the parent's representations, taking them literally, he or she may develop a false or compliant self.

An inner text, on the other hand, might be a dream or fantasy in which the ego or another aspect of the personality (complex, desire, etc.) is presented. If the child over-identifies with the image in the inner text, he or she may be led to act out through an identification with an unconscious image.

The personality may take several possible attitudes toward these representations. The individual might (1) comply with the image and assume the image as his or her conscious identity, and thus develop a *compliant self structure*; (2) adopt a defiant or rebellious attitude toward the image, taking just the opposite position presented by the image, and thus develop a *defiant self structure*; (3) be unconscious of the existence of the image; or (4) view the image as some aspect of inner or outer reality, but not feel that his or her identity is identical with the image. This last position is possible only when the individual has the psychic ability to view his or her images (both inner and outer) as other, thus making it possible for the ego to hold each image at sufficient psychic distance so as not to over-identify with its contents, while at the same time maintaining a feeling relation to it.

Creating a Psychic Sense of Otherness

The capacity for the psyche to see its conscious representation at a distance is the result of the originary differentiation taking place during the mirror stage. This leads to the second consequence of language acquisition: the creation of an inner sense of otherness. The process of acquiring language results in the creation of a second order of being, the textual realm of representation. The post-mirror-stage personality is differentiated into a representational ego and an experiential self. As the child passes through the mirror stage and acquires language, the *internal dynamic* between the representational ego and the experiential self comes into being. By assimilating and being assimilated by language, the speaker increasingly identifies the totality of the psyche with the first-person-singular pronoun. This tendency is particularly evident in relation to dreams. When a person first looks at a dream, the usual reaction is to identify consciousness with the dream-ego and to identify the other persons in the dream with their apparent external referents. For example, the naive dreamer identifies his or her mother image as it appears in a dream with his or her actual mother, thus making no distinction between object-as-such and the image one has of it. Through the analytic process of differentiating the image from its referent, whether 'self' or 'object,' a sense of inner otherness and psychic interiority slowly comes into being. However, as long as the image is identified with its referent, its presence as a distinct psychological entity within the person's psyche will remain unconscious.[20] The conscious mind cannot recognize the relative autonomy of psychic images if the image is projected back onto the referent and confused with the referent's own autonomy.

The Realm of the Unconscious

Through the acquisition of language the child is ushered into an elaborate textual universe, a collective matrix of signifiers. The post-mirror stage child's entrance into this vast realm of symbols creates the internal ego/self dynamic and signals the onset of subjectivity. *But the entrance into the world of symbolic representation opens up an ontological gap between representation and referent, image (visual, acoustic, kinesthetic, etc.) and the unknowable. The exclusion of the experiential self from the realm of representations leads to a third effect of language: the appearance of an unconscious order of experience.* Although textual mediation is necessary for consciousness and self-consciousness, the price paid for such mediation is the creation of a certain unbridgeable distance between text and original lived experience. While psychic images are representations experienced in the sphere of consciousness, the realm of unmediated experience is the realm of the unconscious. And about this subject we cannot speak ....

---

[20] Jung, *CW* 4.

CHAPTER FIVE

Childhood Seduction:
A Crisis in Representation

Is a thought "real"? Probably ... only in so far as it refers to something that can be perceived by the senses. If it does not, it is considered "unreal," "fanciful," "fantastic," etc., and is thus declared nonexistent. This happens all the time in practice, despite the fact that it is a philosophical monstrosity. The thought was and is, even though it refers to no tangible reality; it even has an effect, otherwise no one would have noticed it. But because the little word "is"—to our way of thinking—refers to something material, the "unreal" thought must be content to exist in a nebulous super-reality, which in practice means the same thing as unreality. And yet the thought may have left undeniable traces of its reality behind it. ... Our practical conception of reality would therefore seem to be in need of revision.[1]

—C. G. Jung

In the move from the 20th to the 21st century our relation to the image has undergone dramatic changes. Questioning the integrity of the image has become a postmodern obsession. With this crisis of representation has come an uncertainty as to when the image is to be viewed literally and when it is to be viewed metaphorically. The 'real' and the 'imaginal' have become, at times, almost indistinguishable. Little wonder that with this shift in consciousness the clinical eye has once again focused on child sexual abuse and the problem of differentiating the real event from the imaginal experience.

The Status of Psychic Images

It has been over 100 years since the inception of depth psychology, and the same clinical phenomenon that first preoccupied Freud and Jung has now returned to center stage in professional debates. In the past

---

[1] C. G. Jung, *The Collected Works of C. G. Jung*, tr. R. F. C. Hull, vol. 8 (Princeton: Princeton University Press, 1971), para. 44-745. All subsequent references to Jung's *Collected Works*, abbreviated to *CW*, will be by volume and paragraph number, designated by §.

century, many refinements have been effected in psychological theory, analytic technique, and clinical practice, but we still find ourselves struggling over the nature and status of psychic images. The exact relationship between psychic images, personal history, and psychopathology remains shrouded in mystery. No certitude exists in the profession as to what the patient's psychic image of childhood seduction refers to. One theory reduces the image to a traumatic event in early childhood. Another refers it to an unconscious wish. Yet another approaches the image of seduction as an attempt at integration of unconscious contents directed by the self. And still other theories reduce the image to frame violations, transference and counter-transference dynamics, or archetypal constellations. And the more eclectic approaches view the image from various combinations of the above perspectives.

The current debate over how to approach the role of childhood seduction in personality formation therapeutically stretches between two extremes. On one side, we find those therapists specializing in multiple personality disorder, who approach the patient's psychic images from the perspective of early childhood traumatic events that have become dissociated from the patient's more stable conscious identity. These split-off parts of the psyche begin to live a relatively autonomous existence in the personality, creating conditions ranging from dissociative disorder to multiple personality. On the other side of the controversy, we find the patient's psychic images being approached as the products of false memory syndrome. From this perspective, the fragmentary memories of childhood seduction and abuse are viewed as the patient's desire to separate from the family to which he or she is unconsciously tied. The patient is seen as having intense guilt about separating from the family and unconsciously blames the parents' excessive love for his or her inability to stand alone. This dependency dates back to early childhood and leaves the person with a feeling of hostile dependency on the parents, which in adult life manifests in the form of destructive fantasies of childhood seduction and/or abuse. Through the verbalization of these fantasies, separation from the family is achieved.

This debate over how to interpret psychic images therapeutically strikes at the very heart of depth psychology and cannot simply be turned into a question of what is 'fact' and what is 'fantasy.' The difficulty with this issue—and what makes it so psychologically poignant—is that a certain 'truth' resides subtly on both sides of the debate. Each perspective presents cogent theoretical arguments and graphic clinical examples to defend its position. There are cases where the patient has been physically seduced and abused as a child and later develops a dissociative disorder to cope with this reality. There are, as well, cases where the patient was never touched physically, but as a child was emotionally abused, molested through inappropriate looking and exposed to a family dynamic lacking basic psychic boundaries. In addition, cases exist where the adult patient, out of his or her own confusion and suffering, tells of seduction and abuse that did not literally happen, but through these images the patient is able to integrate psychically the darker side of the family that was never allowed to be experienced literally as a child.

Where does the truth lie in these cases? Does it reside in the material or the immaterial facts? Perhaps it resides in a subtle appreciation of both. More than in any other clinical phenomenon, we witness in 'memories' of childhood seduction the dynamic interaction between the productive and reproductive aspects of psychic imaging. Each patient's psychic images must be believed by the therapist to *contain a certain truth about the reality of his or her personality and developmental history. The difficulty sets in when the therapist attempts to make claims about reality and truth that extend beyond the possibilities of the analytic relationship.* Criminal courts, even with extensive means of research at their disposal, often find it impossible to sort out the 'facts' in these cases. How, then, can we expect the therapist in a closed therapeutic vessel to do what social workers, detectives, lawyers and polygraphs fail to do? And yet, at times, certain therapists do claim to know what is 'real.' *Often this knowledge of 'the real' has been unconsciously imported into the therapeutic encounter through the implicit assumptions contained in the therapist's personal theory of neurosis. And rarely are the therapist's theoretical assumptions subjected to the same careful analysis as the patient's clinical material.*

This chapter will focus on an analysis of the implicit assumptions various psychoanalytic theories import into the therapeutic relationship to explain the etiological significance of memory-images and fantasies of childhood sexual abuse. My intention is *to develop a greater appreciation of how the therapist's theory of neurosis plays a significant role in determining what is experienced as 'real' and 'true' in the clinical encounter by the patient.*

Let's turn to the history of childhood seduction in depth psychology and explore some of the underlying psychotherapeutic assumptions held by the founders of psychoanalysis.

Freud's Seduction Theory

The first significant etiological explanation of neurosis in depth psychology was Freud's seduction theory. To understand the deeper issues motivating Freud's theory, it is necessary to locate the event historically. The dominant theory of neurosis in 1896 claimed 'heredity,' i.e., congenital degeneration with the presence of cerebral lesions, to be the primary cause of hysterical symptoms. The heredity theory considered the parents to be passive transmitters of the disease to the child through genetics. Against this background, Freud developed his new seduction theory in which the parents were now conceived as actively creating hysterical symptoms in the child through seductive actions. Shifting the cause of the neurosis from the forefathers to the 'actual' fathers, Freud wrote: "The foundation for a neurosis would accordingly always be laid in childhood by an adult."[2]

Persons suffering from neurosis, according to the new theory, had been sexually abused as children by their parents, older siblings, or parental substitutes. To account for the transmission of hysteria from generation to generation, Freud formulated the phylogenetic dictum, "heredity is seduction by the father."[3] No longer were the parents viewed as passively transmitting hysteria to their children through genetics. Now, a parental figure was viewed as actively creating hysteria in the child through seductive behavior.

By the spring of 1896, Freud had treated eighteen analytic cases, all of which seemed to confirm his new hypothesis. He developed a therapeutic method based upon this hypothesis, which causally linked the current neurotic symptoms, through a chain of verbal associations, to a past sexual trauma. The seduction theory clearly implicated child sexual abuse, both in its gross and its subtle forms, as being pathogenic and more fundamental in neurotic symptom formation than heredity.

So aware was Freud of his challenge to the heredity theory that in February of 1896 he sent off for publication two papers dealing with the

---

[2] Sigmund Freud, "The Aetiology of Hysteria," *The Standard Edition of the Complete Psychological Works of Sigmund Freud*, vol. III, tr. J. Strachey (London: Hogarth Press, 1962), pp. 208-09. All subsequent references to this work, abbreviated to *SE*, will be by volume and page number.

[3] Sigmund Freud, *The Origins of Psychoanalysis: Letters to Wilhelm Fliess, Drafts and Notes: 1892-1899*, tr. E. Mosbacher & J. Strachey (New York: Basic Books, 1954), p. 180.

dispute over the origin of hysteria. One paper, written for a French publication, criticized the disciples of Charcot, his former teacher, for holding to heredity as the primary etiology of neurosis;[4] the second paper, written for German physicians, presented a similar critique.[5]

Freud's theoretical shift away from heredity and the neuropathological model had already begun in 1893 with his short book entitled *On Aphasia*. There Freud showed that even where there is an organic lesion, the putative source of the aphasic phenomenon of verbal dissociation, the splitting off of one idea from another must be understood independently of the anatomical location of the lesion. This theoretical shift from conceiving verbal pathology as a result of a brain lesion to conceiving it as a result of the splitting off of an idea from consciousness opened the way for Freud to a completely new understanding of hysteria. *Neurotic symptoms result from a splitting occurring in the mind, not in the cerebral cortex.* In hysteria, the mind develops a 'lesion' when a specific idea is cut off from consciousness. If an idea is split off, dissociated from the conscious mind, as in hysteria, then what causes the splitting? What is the origin of the mental lesion?

Freud's answer to this question was ingeniously simple and economical: a mental lesion is created by a psychic 'trauma,' the trauma of childhood seduction. Sexually traumatic events in childhood give rise to mental lesions, i.e., split-off ideas not verbally expressed and remaining outside the realm of consciousness. Later in life, these split-off parts of the mind find expression through neurotic or psychotic symptoms.

Freud's new explanation for the origin of mental lesions, i.e., hysterical symptoms, deliteralizes an older neuropathological idea. *Traditional neurology held that a physical trauma to the head could result in a cerebral lesion. Freud's new theory suggested that a sexual trauma to the child's mind could result in a psychic lesion.*

Deliteralization of Seduction

The origin of psychoanalysis can be read as a deliteralizing of the traditional medical concepts of brain, lesion, and trauma. Freud's progressive deliteralization of medical concepts took a dramatic shift on September 21, 1897, when in a published and much-studied letter,

---

[4] Freud, "Heredity and the Aetiology of the Neuroses," *SE* III, 142-56.
[5] Freud, "Further Remarks on the Neuro-psychoses of Defense," *SE* III, 159-85.

Freud wrote Wilhelm Fliess to confide in him his discovery that some of the stories of childhood seduction by the father as told by his patients were fantasies. This discovery called into question the very foundation of his seduction theory. Perhaps no aspect in the history of psychoanalysis has been more analyzed, more exalted, and more distorted than this letter of September 21, 1897. While many hail it as the origin of psychoanalysis, or condemn it for dismissing the stories of seduction as mere fantasies, it seems few that have actually read Freud's original letter. The ideas contained in this letter have been so distorted through selective editing by Alice Miller, Jeffrey Masson, Milton Klein, and others trying to resurrect the seduction theory that to help clarify the reasons for Freud's decision, we need to read the entire section of the letter dealing with his seduction theory, or the 'neurotica,' as he called it.

21 September 1897

My dear Wilhelm,
Here I am again, arrived yesterday morning, refreshed, cheerful, impoverished, at present without work, and, having settled in again, I am writing to you first.
And now I want to confide in you immediately the great secret of something that in the past few months has gradually dawned on me. I no longer believe in my NEUROTICA. This is probably not intelligible without an explanation; after all, you yourself found what I was able to tell you credible. So I will begin historically and tell you from where the reasons for rejecting it came. The first group of factors were the continual disappointment in my attempts to bring my analyses to a real conclusion; the running away of people who for a time had seemed my most favourably inclined patients, the lack of the complete success on which I had counted, and the possibility of explaining to myself the partial successes in other, familiar, ways. Then there was the astonishing thing that in every case the father, not excluding my own, had to be accused of being perverse, and the unexpected realization of the frequency of hysteria, with precisely the same conditions prevailing in each case, whereas surely such widespread perversions against children are not very probable. (The [incidence] of perversion would have to be immeasurably more frequent than the [resulting] hysteria because the illness, after all, occurs only where there has been an accumulation of events and there is a contributory factor that

weakens the defense.) Then, third, the certain insight that there is no "indication of reality" in the unconscious, so that one cannot distinguish between truth and fiction that has been cathected with affect. (This leaves open the possible explanation that sexual phantasy regularly makes use of the theme of the parents.) Fourthly, there was the consideration that even in the most deep-reaching psychoses the unconscious memory does not break through, so that the secret of infantile experiences is not revealed even in the most confused states of delirium. When one thus sees that the unconscious never overcomes the resistance of the conscious, the expectation diminishes that in treatment the reverse process will take place to the extent that the unconscious is completely tamed by consciousness.

So far was I influenced by these considerations that I was ready to abandon two things—the complete solution of a neurosis and sure reliance on its etiology in infancy. Now I do not know where I am, as I have not succeeded in gaining a theoretical understanding of repression and its interplay of forces. It once again seems arguable that only later experiences give the impetus to phantasies which throw back to childhood; and with this, the factor of an hereditary disposition regains a sphere of influence from which I had made it my business to oust it—in the interest of fully explaining neurosis.

Were I depressed, jaded, unclear in my mind, such doubts might be taken as signs of weakness. But as I am in just the opposite state, I must acknowledge them to be the result of honest and effective intellectual labor, and I am proud that after penetrating so far I am still capable of such criticism. Can these doubts be only an episode on the way to further knowledge? (This translation is a composite of James Strachey's and Jeffrey Masson's earlier translations and my own.)

In the letter Freud gives four sets of reasons for giving up his seduction theory. The first set has to do with his most favorable patients leaving therapy without the analytic treatment producing the therapeutic success he had anticipated. Freud had encountered unexplainable transference and counter-transference reactions. The second set of reasons focuses on his discovery that in every case the patient's current problem was blamed on perverse acts by the father and that the incidence of perversion would have to be much greater than the incidence of hysteria to account for an actual traumatic etiology. Third, and perhaps most important, Freud realizes that there is no "indication of reality" in the unconscious. The phrase "indication of reality" is put in quotation marks so as to remind Fliess of his previous use of the phrase, the "Project for a Scientific Psychology." Two years earlier, in 1895, Freud had used the phrase in the "Project" in the context of a discussion of his second "biological rule of attention." Freud had constructed the rule to account for how the ego differentiates real perceptions from wishes or apperceptions. The actual rule in the "Project" reads: "The indications of discharge or the indications of quality are also primarily indications of 'reality', and are intended to serve the purpose of distinguishing the cathexes of real perceptions from the cathexes of wishes."[6] Freud believed ego-consciousness was capable of qualitatively differentiating real perceptions from wishes and desires based upon the quality of the neurological discharge or cathexes. Whether or not this is neurologically accurate, it was a part of Freud's belief system at the time.

Suddenly, in the fall of 1897, Freud found himself again confronted with the problem of differentiating outer perceptions from inner fantasies and wishes. This time, however, he was dealing not with the ego and its problem of attention, but rather with the unconscious and memory-images. His conclusion in this instance was that in the unconscious there is 'no' "indication of reality." This realization led Freud to write in his letter of September 21 that: "it is impossible to distinguish between truth and emotionally-charged fiction." If this is the case, Freud reasoned, then emotionally-charged inner sexual desires can regularly make use of memory-images of the outer parents.

The final reason Freud presents for giving up his seduction theory and a therapy based on bringing to consciousness the person's "outer" childhood history is the realization that even in the most acute psychoses and states of delirium, all the memories of outer infantile experiences do not surface. Therefore, the goal of therapy cannot be to recover all of one's childhood memories completely.

Based on these four considerations, Freud expanded—not abandoned as has been charged—his previous etiology of neurosis, so as to include the role of fantasy in symptom-formation. On April 27, 1898, he wrote to Fliess: "Initially I defined the etiology too narrowly; the share of fantasy in it is far greater than I had thought in the beginning."[7]

---

[6] Freud, *Origins of Psychoanalysis*, p. 429.
[7] Freud, *Origins of Psychoanalysis*, p. 429.

The Expanded Etiology

In expanding his etiology, Freud did not abandon the awareness that actual, historical seductions occur, nor did he abandon the idea of seduction as a psychic reality. Rather, he acknowledged that fantasies of seduction could appear in memory, even when no physical seduction has taken place. The child can psychologically be seduced by the desire of the external other, or the internal other, even in the absence of physical acts. The significance of this discovery can and has been distorted, but it cannot be over-emphasized. *For Freud had discovered that memory records not only perceptions, but also wishes and apperceptions. Memory is a record of the events occurring in the exterior environment confabulated with those events occurring in the interior environment.* Furthermore, in the unconscious there is no "indication of reality," therefore in previously unconscious memory images, it is impossible to distinguish between history and fantasy.

Freud's new theory posited the existence of a psychic life of fantasy, in large part unconscious, co-existing in the personality along with memories of actual historical events. These fantasy-images Freud derived ontogenetically from the unfolding of instinctual drives and apperceived bodily feelings. In the Id, these erotic and aggressively toned fantasy images commingle with historical memory images; their dynamic interrelation with the parental imagoes Freud termed the Oedipus complex. His new theory viewed the Oedipus complex and the vicissitudes of Id psychology as the primary, though not the only, motivating forces structuring the personality. The role of the outer environment was never denied by Freud. *But, the problem for Freud, and later for Jung, was how to explain the fact that many adults suffer childhood seduction, yet only certain individuals subsequently develop psychic disturbances. And likewise, certain adults who have never been sexually molested as children, but who later fantasize about being molested, also develop these same psychic disorders.* As to whether the actual seduction or the fantasized seduction has a greater pathogenic effect, Freud wrote, "We have not succeeded in pointing to any difference in the consequences, whether phantasy or reality has the greater share."[8]

Freud never denied the reality of his patients' memories of actual childhood traumas, as some writers have suggested. Rather, he recognized

---

[8] Freud, *Origins of Psychoanalysis*, p. 429.

that the memories of actual childhood are continually being confabulated with unconscious fantasies and, in the context of the closed analytic vessel, it is almost impossible to distinguish which aspects of unconscious images refer to outer objective perceptions and which refer to inner desires and fantasies.

Jung's Etiology

Jung wrote an early paper on the function of childhood memories in the etiology of neurosis, which is particularly significant to our discussion. The paper, entitled "The Theory of Psychoanalysis," consists of seven lectures given in September 1912 at Fordham University Medical School. The essay is nearly 150 pages in length and some of the more relevant sub-sections are entitled: "The Theory of Sexual Trauma in Childhood," "The Predisposition for the Trauma," "The Sexual Element in the Trauma," "Infantile Sexual Fantasy," "Unconscious Fantasy Systems," "The Oedipus Complex," "The Etiology of Neurosis," and "The Etiological Significance of the Actual Present." Discussing the etiological significance of historical traumata and their relation to imaginary traumata, Jung writes:

> We are thus obliged to assume that many traumata in early infancy are of a purely fantastic nature, mere fantasies in fact, while others do have objective reality. With this discovery, somewhat bewildering at first sight, the etiological significance of the sexual trauma in childhood falls to the ground, as it now appears totally irrelevant whether the trauma really occurred or not. Experience shows us that fantasies can be just as traumatic in their effects as real traumata. ... We know very well that there are a great many more people who experience traumata in childhood or adult life without getting a neurosis. Therefore the trauma, other things being equal, has no absolute etiological significance and will pass off without having any lasting effect. From this simple reflection it is perfectly clear that the individual must meet the trauma with a quite definite inner predisposition in order to make it really effective. This inner predisposition is not to be understood as that obscure, hereditary disposition of which we know so little, but as a psychological development which reaches its climax, and becomes manifest, at the traumatic moment.[9]

---

[9] Jung, *CW* 4 § 216- 217.

We must remember that at the time this was written the prevailing etiologies located the determining factors either internally in the form of hereditary predisposition or environmentally in the form of actual childhood traumata. Both Freud and Jung were working to formulate a new etiological vision, locating the determining factors midway between the environment and the personal psychology of the patient. In discussing the prevailing explanations and his new epigenetic etiology, Jung writes:

> It is the fashion nowadays to regard all mental abnormalities not of exogenous origin as consequences of hereditary degeneration, and not as essentially *conditioned by the psychology of the patient and his environment* [emphasis added]. But this is an extreme view which fails to do justice to the facts. We know very well how to find the middle course in dealing with the etiology of tuberculosis. There are undoubtedly cases of tuberculosis where the germ of the disease proliferates from early childhood in soil predisposed by heredity, so that even under the most favorable conditions the patient cannot escape his fate. But there are also cases where there is no hereditary taint and no predisposition, and yet a fatal infection occurs. This is equally true of the neuroses, where things will not be radically different from what they are in general pathology. An extreme theory about predisposition will be just as wrong as an extreme theory about environment.[10]

Jung's approach opts for an epigenetic etiology midway between Aristotle's empiricism and Plato's nativism. This hypothesis means the pathogenic experience occurring in the outer environment, for example, a childhood seduction, is supplemented by an inner psychological factor. *A combination of outer history and inner emotional response determines the pathogenesis.*

Confluence of History and Emotion

Material history and emotional reactions come together in memory. To retrieve the historical events of childhood, the analyst must rely on the patient's memory of what happened. In the course of analysis, memories in various forms are continually being analyzed. These memory-images may be of the previous analytic session, the events of

---

[10] Jung, *CW* 4 § 209.

the past week, a recent dream, a story about the patient's parents, or an event from childhood. Memories are images arising from a conjunction of outer environmental influences and the specific emotional reactions of the individual. The memory image, therefore, reflects any actual historical event with very considerable qualification. Jung referred to the composite memory-image as an imago. The imago is a distinct psychological entity which exists independently of the historical referent, even if based in part on perception.

Just here the difficulty arises. As long as the image is identified with the actual behavior of the object in the outer world, for example, the erotically aroused father-imago identified with the actual father, the presence of the image as a distinct psychological entity within the patient's personality will remain unconscious. The conscious mind cannot recognize the relative autonomy of composite images, because the images are projected back onto the object world and confused with the object's own autonomy. Psychic reality is fused with physical reality; the finger pointing at the moon is confused with the moon itself; the world of images is identified with the world of material history. In short: the object contaminates the image. In painting, the distinction between object and imago has been ingeniously portrayed by René Magritte. His painting of a green meerschaum pipe is entitled (in English translation): "This is not a pipe."

The realization of the psychological importance in analysis of differentiating the object from its imago led Jung to speak no longer only of historical childhood and historical parents, but to also employ the term "imago." Jung discusses the reason for this decision in the following section from his Fordham University lectures:

> Among the things that were of the utmost significance at the infantile period the most influential are the personalities of the parents. Even when the parents have long been dead and lost, or should have lost, all significance, the situation of the patient having perhaps completely changed since then, they are still somehow present and as important as if they were still alive. The patient's love, admiration, resistance, hatred, and rebelliousness still cling to their effigies, transfigured by affection or distorted by envy, and often bearing little resemblance to the erstwhile reality. It was this fact that compelled me to speak no longer of "father" and "mother" but to employ instead the term "imago", because these

fantasies are not concerned any more with real father and mother but with subjective and often very much distorted images of them which lead a shadowy but nonetheless potent existence in the patient's mind.[11]

The imago bears traces of both external and internal history. Impressions of the external world entering via the perceptual systems are affected by the particular emotional reactions of the perceiver. The person's love, admiration, resistance, hatred, rebelliousness, envy transfigures the perceptual contents, producing an imago. The perceiver's emotional reactions are recorded in memory through the transfigurations of the actual perceptual contents.

The 'imago' is the merging place of perception and apperception. When confronted with the realization that *from the perspective of the imago there can never be complete separation of history and fantasy,* perception from apperception (and in many instances it is impossible to determine whether or not there was actual physical abuse), we cannot but conclude that, whenever there is abuse reported by patients, some form of 'abuse' is present. The therapist must believe the patient's story—regardless of whether it is based on material or immaterial facts. Hearing the story as historical remembering does not necessarily make it more "real"—except in those cases where the person's *Weltanschauung* requires history to authenticate reality. And we must keep in mind that certain patients or therapists may need to experience an image in the form of a historical memory in order for that image to be felt as a real happening.

The problem is not whether or not the patient suffers from childhood seduction or abuse. Of course the patient does, and such abuse exist simply because the patient says it exists. The abuse exists as a psychic fact. The real problem lies in how the treating therapist approaches the patient's image. Furthermore, *how the analyst enters the image therapeutically will reveal the analyst's own unconscious working definition of reality and theory of neurosis.*

If the therapist derives psychic reality from the physical and the historical, then physical, historical seduction will be considered the preponderant etiological factor. If, however, the therapist defines

---

[11] Jung, *CW* 4 § 305.

psychic reality more in terms of wishes, desires, and archetypal images, then these factors will be considered more etiologically significant. And, finally, if the therapist works from the definition of reality that *both* the environment and the individual emotional responses of the person are equally real, then a combination of these factors will determine the etiology.

From this perspective the problematics of abuse become paradigmatic for understanding the therapist's sense of psychic reality. Staying with the imago, that merging place of perception and apperception, historical autobiography and emotionally charged fiction, keeps the analyst and patient always *in* psychic reality and aware of the primacy in analysis of this reality over all other realities.

Jung's theory of interpretation based upon an objective and a subjective level provides a therapeutic method for working with this interaction between history and fantasy. The objective level refers the imago to the outer historical event and interpersonal relationships through the process of free association. The subjective level, on the other hand, refers the same psychic image to inner events and intrapsychic dynamics. The therapeutic movement between objective and subjective levels encourages the individual to confront both the reality of the environment and outer history as well as the reality of subjective imaginings and emotional responses.

The Psychology of Rumor

Between 1910 and 1911, Jung again dealt with the problem of childhood sexuality and the intermingling of objective and subjective history. This time he approached the problem from the perspective of social dynamics. His essay, "A Contribution to the Psychology of Rumor," was prompted by a request from the local school authorities for Jung to examine the mental status of a thirteen-year-old high school girl.[12] The student had been expelled from school after her male teacher had overheard an ambiguous sexual story involving him being told by some of his female students. Investigation revealed that Marie, the student referred to Jung, had told three of her classmates a dream she had had involving this teacher. The dream itself contained nothing scandalous, but as the dream

---

[12] Jung, *CW* 4 § 95-128.

began to circulate from student to student, each new narrator unconsciously supplemented the narrative with elements from her own unconscious fantasies and unresolved complexes. Jung presents eight different versions of the dream collected from various students. The altered dream texts arose from a conjunction of objective elements from the original narrative intertwined with subjective elements supplied by the new narrators. His analysis of the progressive transformation of the dream text into a rumor disclosed how unconscious sexual complexes lying dormant in each new narrator were 'detonated' by the emotionally toned story. The analysis of the various versions of the story revealed that the secondary elaborations supplied by the re-tellers of the dream, actually functioned to interpret the latent content of the dream itself. Jung concludes:

> So far as the interpretation of the dream is concerned, there is nothing for me to add; the children themselves have done all that is necessary, leaving practically nothing over for psychoanalytic interpretation. *The rumor has analyzed and interpreted the dream.*[13]

Jung's method of analyzing the sexual rumor is particularly instructive. He approaches the events from the perspective of psychological understanding. His analysis is not based upon the constructs of true or false, fact or fantasy, good or bad, guilty or innocent, victim or victimizer. Rather, he starts simply with the reality of the phenomenon itself and attempts to understand its meaning psychologically. *His analysis of the transformations of the original dream text into a rumor through the constellation of the dormant complexes in the re-tellers provides a powerful insight into the evolution of a historical narrative in relation to interpersonal and intrapsychic dynamics.*

For a better understanding of today's clinical perspective on the effect of childhood sexual abuse on the adult personality, let us review briefly some of the current research on the long-term impact of child sexual abuse.

---

[13] Jung, *CW* 4 § 125.

The Empirical Perspective

The most comprehensive review of the research to date is by Angela Browne and David Finkelhor, and it focuses directly on the effect in adult life of childhood sexual abuse. Their research examines three important issues: (1) the incidence of psychopathology in relation to age groups; (2) whether the sexual trauma is the only etiological factor, or whether there is a pre-morbid factor already in the child's environment; and (3) the general public's "adulto-centric" tendency to view abuse from the perspective of "long-term impact."

In regard to the incidence of psychopathology in relation to age groups, the research found that "seventeen percent of 4 to 6 year-olds in the study met the criteria for 'significant pathology,' demonstrating more overall disturbance than a normal population but less than the norms for other children their age who were in psychiatric care. The highest incidence of psychopathology was found in the 7 to 13 year-old group, with 40 percent scoring in the seriously disturbed range. Interestingly, few of the adolescent victims were found to exhibit severe psychopathology."[14] The research found that sexual abuse between the ages of 7 and 13 produced the highest incidence of clinically significant psychopathology.

Second, concerning the possibility of a pre-morbid factor brought into the traumatic experience by the child, the study notes:

> One of the most imposing challenges for researchers is to explore the sources of trauma in sexual abuse. Some of the apparent effects of sexual abuse may be due to premorbid conditions, such as family conflict or emotional neglect, that actually contribute to a vulnerability to abuse and to exacerbating later trauma. Other effects may be due less to the experience itself than to later social reactions to disclosure.[14]

The research confirmed the earlier views of Freud and Jung that the source of the trauma in sexual abuse is a combination of environmental factors plus the specific emotional reaction of the child.

Third, regarding the public's preoccupation with the long-term effects of childhood abuse, the study's concluding paragraph states:

---

[14] Angela Browne & David Finkelhor, "Impact of Child Sexual Abuse: A Review of the Research," *Psychological Bulletin* 99.1 (1986): 68.

> Finally, there is an unfortunate tendency in interpreting the effects of sexual abuse (as well as in studies of other childhood trauma) to over-emphasize long-term impact as the ultimate criterion. Effects seem to be considered less "serious" if their impact is transient and disappears in the course of development. However, this tendency to assess everything in terms of its long-term effect betrays an "adulto-centric" bias. Adult traumas such as rape are not assessed ultimately in terms of whether they will have an impact on old age; they are acknowledged to be painful and alarming events, whether their impact lasts one year or ten. Similarly, childhood traumas should not be dismissed because no "long-term effects" can be demonstrated. Child sexual abuse needs to be recognized as a serious problem of childhood, if only for the immediate pain, confusion and upset that can ensue.[15]

The research of Browne and Finkelhor presents a descriptive analysis of the impact, the *effect*, of child sexual abuse, but it does not analyze the cause or etiology of the syndrome.

Etiology and the Treatment of Choice

At the beginning of treatment, the therapist is often confronted with the question of etiology. Therapy begins with a differentiation of the patient's presenting symptoms followed by a consideration of the possible cause or etiology of the symptoms. Choice of treatment may then derive from how the therapist answers the etiological question. The answer to the question of etiology will more often than not be influenced decisively by the therapist's own theoretical commitment—a commitment which implicitly dictates what the major determinants of personality are and where they are located. If, for example, the therapist views the major determinants of personality to be located in the outer world, then he or she will look to the patient's actual parents and siblings, bi-personal events, childhood environment, and history for the etiology of the patient's symptoms. If, however, the therapist's theoretical commitment views the major determinants of personality to be located in the inner world, then he or she will look to the patient's Oedipus complex, unconscious drives, typology, complexes, or archetypal images for explanation. The analyst's theoretical commitment has a significant

---

[15] Browne & Finkelhor, p. 76.

impact on counter-transference reactions, as well as on patients' attitudes toward their own symptoms and personal histories. If the analyst's theoretical orientation governs what will be viewed as the pathogenic factors in the patient's personality, then what determines the analyst's choice of theory?

Theory and Types

Jung has suggested that the analyst's choice of theory is partially a result of typology. Extraverts will place greater determining significance on the environmental and objective factors, introverts on the interior and subjective factors. Jung's theory of types attempts to understand psychologically the theoretical differences between Freud and Adler. The theory of types was an ingenious attempt to differentiate the various epistemological constraints imposed by consciousness upon the process of knowing. Interestingly enough, Jung's theory is itself grounded in the introverted perspective, locating the determining factors inside the individual in the form of typological predisposition.

While his analysis focused on those constraints which govern and limit our capacity to know, Jung neglected a second set of constraints which arise from the analyst's implicit ontological commitment. An ontological commitment can be defined simply as the analyst's working definition of reality. A short children's story from Persia, narrated to me many years ago by Gitta Malek-Nasrie, may help clarify what I mean.

> In Iran a series of children's stories tell about a holy man called Mullah Nasrudin, a sort of Persian counterpart of Uncle Remus. One day Mullah Nasrudin's friends were walking around when suddenly Mullah Nasrudin galloped past them on his horse, apparently looking for something. A short time later, Mullah Nasrudin again galloped past them. This happened several more times, at which point his friends decided to stop and offer to help him in his search. So, when Mullah Nasrudin again came galloping by, his friends stopped him and asked what he was looking for. To this, Mullah Nasrudin replied: "I am looking for my horse."

Our unconscious definition of reality is the horse on which our conscious perspective is mounted. There is, perhaps, no animal that carries more psychic weight, bears more burdens, and takes over the reins and rides away with us more often than our ontology. Our ontological commitment is the fantasy of reality we are unconsciously moved by and which constrains our sense of reality, determining what will be experienced literally and what metaphorically.

The relationship between theory formation and the constraints of being (ontology) and knowing (epistemology) can be imagined as a house built on a lot, with a foundation and many upper stories. The house with its different stories is like the tradition of depth psychology, with its different theoretical narratives. The foundation, a ground floor through which you must pass, and which supports all the various upper stories, is the epistemology. To get at any clinical and empirical data whatsoever, we must pass through an implicit theory of knowledge, and, therefore, the limitations of the human mind and its capacity to know.

Jung's theory of psychological types and the four functions of consciousness are an elaborate differentiation of the various types of epistemological constraints making up the structures of consciousness. While Jung tried to expose the various foundations of knowledge upon which psychological theories are built, he neglected an analysis of the ground upon which the theory itself is built. This ground is called Being or Reality and the study of its ground rules is ontology. All the various theories of knowledge and all the stories built upon them are grounded on a more fundamental level, in a working definition of reality. This unshakeable definition of reality determines the elements in the patient's symptomatology and history, which from the therapist's point of view, cannot be seen through, deliteralized. These are the so-called literal realities of the case history not reducible to some more fundamental reality.

Multiple Etiologies

The etiology of personality structure and its associated psychopathologies has been dominated by three dramatically different explanatory constructs. Whether one is committed to Aristotle's empiricism, Plato's nativism, or the current epigenetic variants, the strategy for introducing change therapeutically into the personality is the same: *for change to occur, therapy must alter the structure of the constraints that harness the personality.* If the constraints are postulated to be in the environment, then therapeutic change will be imagined as changing the environmental schedules. This is the therapeutic strategy adopted by behaviorism. If the constraints are imagined to be located at the physiological level, then therapeutic change will be imagined as changing the interior structures of the person's biochemistry through psychopharmacology. This therapeutic strategy underlies the traditional medical model. And if the constraints are imagined to be located at the interaction between the individual and the environment, then therapeutic change will be imagined as altering this interactional relationship. This strategy is the one adopted by depth psychology. Therapy from this third perspective focuses on changing the relationship between consciousness and the inner environment of unconscious drives and fantasy images, or object-relations with the outer environment. The different schools of thought making up depth psychology differ over which element in the interactional field is viewed as primary, and therefore carries the most etiological significance.

As an exercise in etiological explanation, however, all the above approaches suffer from the regress problem. These theories locate the constraints structuring the personality either in the environment, or in the physiology of the person, or in the interaction between consciousness and the interior and/or exterior environments. The regress problem arises when the theorist tries to account for the origin of the constraints themselves. For example, if we take the behaviorist perspective and view the origin of the environmental constraints as a function of a larger organized environment, then that environment must in turn be organized by an even larger context, which is in turn organized by an even larger one, *ad infinitum*. The behaviorist's etiology lapses into an environmental regress.

This type of explanation when applied to the behavioral pattern of childhood sexual abuse runs something like this: child abuse is caused by the abuser having been sexually abused as a child, by another abuser, who had also been abused as a child, all the way back to the primal horde. In other words, if the therapist's definition of reality is such that only the physical environment is imagined to be most real and etiologically significant, then the therapist will look to the physical environment to find 'the real' cause of the disorder.

When this same problem is approached from the interior physiological perspective of the medical model, then the origin of the constraints will be looked for on the biochemical level in the form of an endocrine, hormone, or some other biochemical imbalance. This etiology will also lapse into the regress problem, because the biochemical explanation regresses onto its design principles, genetics, which again regresses the problem back onto previous generations, without ever accounting for the origin of the genetic code.

If the therapist's working definition of reality views the inter-relation between consciousness and the person's fantasies as primary, then an etiology of child abuse will begin with those constraints innate to the interaction between consciousness and psychic images. On the level of Jung's imago, these constraints will be viewed as a function of a more 'abstract' set of constraints—the archetype-as-such—which is a function of the psyche's innate capacity to create images or phylogenetically determined patterns of behavior. This etiology lapses into an archetypal regress, halting only by accounting for the origin of the behavior through an appeal to the innateness hypothesis. On the other interactional-drive level (early Freud), the fantasy-images are reduced to representations of drives which are then posited as innate first principles. This construct also regresses on to the innateness hypothesis.

Neither is the problem solved by opting for an object-relations or bi-personal approach. In these approaches, the constraints are located either between subjective consciousness and the so-called objective world, or in the intersubjective space. These approaches also lapse into the regress problem, for they cannot account for the origin of the structures in the representational world (Winnicott, Kernberg, Kohut, *et al.*), language (Lacan), or the bi-personal field (Searles, Langs, and Goodheart).

In other words, *we simply have no adequate theory for the origin of the complex structures making up the personality and its psychopathology.* Most etiological explanations are merely new descriptions of the clinical phenomenon, not true explanations. And these causal clinical "explanations" often function as self-serving confirmations of the researcher's unconscious ontological and theoretical commitments. A true explanation, must account for the emergence of new structural properties, or, in this case, syndromes and patterns of behavior. The inability to establish with certainty the etiology of psychiatric syndromes led the editors of the *DSM–IV* to omit etiologies from the manual except where it is indicated in the name of the syndrome itself.

The principle of "causality" is so basic to the idea of etiology and clinical thinking that rarely is it reflected on or called into question. Since Newton, the Western mind has taken for granted that causality implies a logical and temporal priority of cause to effect. In the *Will To Power*, Nietzsche argues that the idea of causal structure is not something given as such, but rather, *the product of a precise tropological or rhetorical operation*, a "chronologische Umdrehung" (chronological reversal). Suppose, for example, a patient feels a pain. This causes the patient or doctor to look for a cause. Seeing a traumatic event in the patient's historical past, the doctor posits a link and reverses the perceptual or phenomenal order, pain ... traumatic event, to produce a causal sequence, *traumatic event ... pain*. Nietzsche concludes:

> The fragment of the outside world of which we become conscious comes after the effect that has been produced on us and is projected 'a posteriori' as its 'cause'. In the phenomenalism of the 'inner world' we invent the chronology of cause and effect. The basic fact of 'inner experience' is that the cause gets *imagined* [emphasis added] after the effect has occurred.[16]

The causal scheme is produced by a metalepsis, a substitution of cause for effect. Causality is the product of a tropological operation, not an indubitable foundation.

Let us be as specific as possible as to what this simple example implies for clinical etiologies. It does not lead to the conclusion that causality is invalid as an explanatory principle. On the contrary, causality is an essential category of the Western psyche. While we cannot escape it, we can become conscious of the circularity built into its internal logic. For example, consider the following succession of events: An experience of pain *causes* the discovery of an antecedent trauma which in turn *causes the production of a cause*. The concept of causation comes with its own internal logic, a tropological structure that unconsciously orders experiences in a very precise way. *The internal structure of causation itself is such that it causes the production of a cause*. This can become problematic if the therapist unconsciously believes that through the use of the notion of causation he or she will discover '*the truth*' about the patient's personality and suffering. As clinicians, we must not forget that 'causation' is also a metaphor with its own precise tropological structure.

---

[16] Friedrich Nietzsche, *Werke Grossoktavausgabe,* vol. 3 (Leipzig: Kroner, 1901), p. 804.

These questions concerning the analyst's epistemology and ontology and the influence they have on the etiological explanation of clinical phenomena may seem far removed from the so-called real clinical issues of child sexual abuse. But when trying responsibly to determine whether certain events actually occurred in outer reality and what consequence these events may have on the structures of the personality, these questions are simply unavoidable. To gain empirical and clinical knowledge, and to attempt to determine what is real and what is the etiology of the syndrome, the treating therapist must consciously, or, as is more often the case, unconsciously adopt a theory of knowledge and make an ontological commitment. These unconscious background assumptions affect the development of the therapist's working etiology of the disorder, the treatment of choice, and the patient's understanding of his or her suffering. And, rarely, if ever, are these unconscious background assumptions made part of the clinical record or of the empirical research.

Today, more than 100 years after the inception of depth psychology, our clinical eye once again focuses in on the problem of childhood seduction and its role in symptom formation. It has taken a full century for clinicians to realize that we need not only to analyze our patient's personal and family dynamics in relation to psychic images of sexual abuse and trauma, but, equally important is to do an in-depth analysis of our own particular clinical theories and the impact their unconscious assumptions have on the interpretation of our patient's clinical material.

CHAPTER SIX

The Legacy of the Dead

What I have to tell about the hereafter, and about death, consists entirely of memories, of images in which I have lived and of thoughts which have buffeted me. These memories in a way also underlie my works; for the latter are fundamentally nothing but attempts, ever renewed, to give an answer to the question of the interplay between the "here" and the 'hereafter." Yet I have never written expressly about a life after death. ... Even now I can do no more than tell stories—"mythologize." Perhaps one has to be close to death to acquire the necessary freedom to talk about it. It is not that I wish we had a life after death. In fact, I would prefer not to foster such ideas. Still, I must state, to give reality its due, that, without my wishing and without my doing anything about it, thoughts of this nature move about in me. I can't say whether these thoughts are true or false, but I do know they are there, and can be given utterance. ... I lend an attentive ear to the strange myths of the psyche, and a careful look at the varied events that come my way, regardless of whether or not they fit in with my theoretical perspective.[1]

—C. G. Jung

As Jung approached his own death in the late 1950s, he became more expressive of the inner working of his psyche. Many close friends passed away during this period and his dreams were frequently inhabited by images of lost associates and loved ones. He had never written about the *idea* of life after death, but Jung now found himself increasingly confronted with images of the dead. The care and sensitivity with which he struggled to understand the significance of this phenomenon provides a remarkable insight into the role lived time plays in psychological understanding.

Mathematics has a category of equations that factor time into their calculations, called differential equations. Unfortunately, psychoanalysis has nothing analogous, no means for integrating time into our clinical

---

[1] C. G. Jung, *Memories, Dreams, Reflections*, ed. Anelia Jaffé, tr. R. & C. Winston (New York: Vintage Books, 1963), pp. 299-300. (Hereafter abbreviated to *MDR*.)

understanding. We often speak about psychic images as if they were divorced from time. As we age, our sense of time qualitatively changes in significant ways. What is viewed literally at one point in the human life cycle may appear increasingly metaphorical at another time. We must not forget that our therapeutic hermeneutic and its relation to the literal and the metaphoric is always embedded in our temporal experience. To gain a better understanding of how *lived time affects psychological understanding*, we will carefully study how Jung's interpretation of "spirits of the dead" transforms over the course of his lifetime.

The 'Ghost' of the Father

In 1896, Jung was studying medicine at the University of Basel when his father unexpectedly died after a short illness. Jung was 21 years old at the time. Six weeks later, he had the following dream, in which his deceased father appeared:

> Suddenly he stood before me and said that he was coming back from his holiday. He had made a good recovery and was now coming home. I thought he would be annoyed with me for having moved into his room. But not a bit of it! Nevertheless, I felt ashamed because I had imagined he was dead. Two days later the dream was repeated. My father had recovered and was coming home, and again I reproached myself because I had thought he was dead.[2]

This dream had a profound effect on Jung. He kept asking himself what it meant that his father returns in dreams and appears so real? The dream forced Jung for the first time to think seriously about the significance of the dead in psychic life.

Somnambulism and Spirits of the Departed

Five years after the death of his father, Jung began work on his medical dissertation, entitled "On the Psychology and Pathology of the So-Called Occult Phenomena."[3] At the beginning of the 20th century, somnambulism, a dissociative disorder, was one of the most studied clinical conditions in psychiatry. Morton Prince in the United States,

---

[2] Jung, *MDR*, p. 96.
[3] C. G. Jung, *The Collected Works of C. G. Jung*, tr. R. F. C. Hull, vol. 1 (Princeton: Princeton University Press, 1971). All subsequent references to Jung's *Collected Works*, abbreviated to *CW*, will be by volume and paragraph number, designated by §.

F. W. H. Myers in England, and Theodore Flournoy in Switzerland all published major studies of the syndrome. In 1901, when Jung was faced with choosing a topic for his dissertation, he settled on a clinical study of several cases of somnambulism.

The first case he presents is of Miss E., a 40-year-old single woman who worked as a bookkeeper in a large business. She enjoyed reasonably good health until age 38, when her physical and psychological condition began to deteriorate. Following a series of family difficulties accompanied by increased stress at work, she began to manifest symptoms of a dissociative disorder Jung diagnosed as somnambulism.

Miss E.'s first significant episode occurred a few days prior to hospitalization. While she was walking with her friend in a cemetery, Miss E. suddenly became extremely emotional and began to tear flowers out of the ground and scratch at the gravestones. Several days later, her friend became concerned about her behavior and took her to the Bürgholzli Klinik in Zürich for a psychiatric evaluation. Outside the hospital, Miss E. encountered three boys whom she described as "three dead people she had dug up." She wanted to go to the neighboring cemetery, but Miss E. was persuaded by her friend, instead, to enter the clinic. She presented her personal history and the events of the past few days to a psychiatrist.

Miss E. was admitted, and during a subsequent night she reported seeing her room full of dead people looking like skeletons. This experience did not frighten her, but she was rather surprised the attendant did not also see 'the dead.' The following night Miss E. reported hearing "the dead children in the adjoining cemetery crying out that they had been buried alive. She wanted to go and dig them up but allowed herself to be restrained."[4] Jung goes on to document the appearance of "spirits of the dead" as the dominant feature of her hallucinations.

The symptoms presented by Miss E. were reminiscent of those clinical conditions earlier described by Richard von Krafft-Ebing as protracted states of hysterical delirium. In his *Textbook on Psychiatry*, Krafft-Ebing indicates that the most frequent visual hallucinations in somnambulism are funerals and processions filled with corpses, devils, and ghosts.

---

[4] Jung, *CW* 1 § 7.

Jung summarizes another similar case in the following way: "A girl of 17, also a severe hysteric. In her attacks she always saw the corpse of her dead mother approaching her, as if to draw her to itself."[5] The focus of Jung's dissertation is a long case study of his cousin, Helly, who also suffered from somnambulism. She was a medium. Jung carefully documented her symptoms and the content of her dialogues during trance states. Her somnambulistic utterances consisted primarily of dialogues with spirits of dead relatives. Helly characterized her experiences of these states, in the following way:

> I do not know if what the spirits say and teach me is true, nor do I know if they really are the people they call themselves; but that my spirits exist is beyond question. I see them before me, I can touch them. I speak to them about everything I wish as naturally as I'm talking to you. They must be real.[6]

Jung's earliest publications in psychiatry at the turn of the century document the appearance of "spirits of the dead" as one of the dominant contents of his patients' hallucinations. How are ghosts and ancestral spirits related to nineteenth-century psychiatry and the origins of depth psychology?

Ghosts and spirits have haunted the Western psyche since its beginning. Greek, Roman, Medieval, and Renaissance literature and theology are rich in examples of the ambivalent role spirits of the dead have played in human experience. From Homer and Sophocles to Chaucer and Shakespeare we find the same theme: The living struggling to make peace with the dead. What is the significance of this *realm between the living and the dead* and why are the dead so intent upon getting our attention?

The Holy Ghost and the Grateful Dead

In his 1983 Eranos lecture entitled, "The Holy Ghost and the Grateful Dead," David L. Miller presented a remarkable analysis of the theological controversies in the West over the past 500 years with respect to the ambivalent place ghosts have held in Christian

---

[5] Jung, *CW* 1 § 14.
[6] Jung, *CW* 1 § 43.

theology.[7] In particular, he reviewed the way in which in the 16th century "Holy Ghost" (Greek *hagion pneuma*) was systematically mistranslated in the King James Version of the Bible to reduce the number of references to ghosts. Through this linguistic sleight-of-hand, Miller notes, the translators began subtly to do away with the "place" between the living and the dead in theology and everyday religious experience. This place had, at various times in the history of Western theology, been inhabited by ghosts, dreams, and the imagination.

The systematic reduction in the use of the translation "Holy Ghost" in the King James Bible, coupled with the emergence of Puritanism in England, Miller argues, led to a theological doctrine of other-worldliness that contained only god and the devil. Those intermediate beings, ghosts and ancestral spirits who moved between the material world and the divine, were banished from Reformation theology in England. This attempt by organized religion to exorcise its theology of ghosts, Miller demonstrates, resulted in a compensatory phenomenon in the secular world. No sooner had the ghost of the Holy Ghost been driven from the new translation of the Bible and Puritan theology than it began to haunt the secular world in a remarkable proliferation of ghost stories. While the realm of intermediate beings was being displaced from mainstream Western theology, it continued to flourish on the margins in folklore, alchemy, and literature, eventually finding its way in the twentieth century into the realm of depth psychology.

Land of the Dead

What in earlier times had been known as the 'land of the dead,' or 'the underworld,' reappears in modern depth psychology as 'the unconscious.' The historical transformation of the 'land of the dead' into depth psychology's notion of 'the unconscious' has been explored in detail by James Hillman in his remarkable book, *The Dream and the Underworld*. Not only does Hillman turn a psychological eye towards the history of the land of the dead, but he also uses the ghostly underworld as a marginal perspective from which to re-examine our basic notions of depth psychology.

---

[7] For a published version of the lecture, see David L. Miller, *Hells and Holy Ghosts: A Theopoetics of Christian Belief* (New Orleans: Spring Journal Books, 2004), pp. 121-129 (Chapter 12: "The Grateful Dead: The Ghosts of Folkore").

Jung first encountered spirits of the dead in his own dreams, and later, at the Bürgholzli Klinik, discovered them in his patients' symptoms. By 1911, these ghostly figures began to appear in his theoretical formulations as well. In his Fordham University lectures, Jung starts to assimilate the function of the dead into his psychological understanding of the very nature of personality, writing the following: "Even when the parents have long been dead and have lost, or should have lost, all significance ... they are still somehow present and as important as if they were still alive."[8] The psychic image, or parental complex, functions like a revenant, living a shadowy but potent existent in the person's psyche.

Imagoes and Revenants

Jung's new conception of psychic images approaches the imago as a distinct psychological entity, existing in the psyche, independent of the historical referent, and yet clearly related to it. The parental imago is like a ghost, related to the deceased person, and yet, existing autonomously of the corpse, its historical referent. In 1916, Jung further expands on the relation between spirits and parental imagoes, this time drawing the analogy between spirits of the dead in traditional societies and the activity of unconscious complexes as described in depth psychology. Jung writes:

> Nearly everything that the primitive says about the tricks which the spirits play on the living, and the general picture they give of the revenants corresponds down to the last detail with the phenomena established by spiritualistic experience. And just as the communications from the "beyond" can be seen to be the activities of broken-off bits of psyche, so these primitive spirits are manifestations of unconscious complexes. ... When the parents die, the projected image goes on working as though it were a spirit existing on its own. The primitive then speaks of parental spirits who return by night ('revenants'), while the modern man calls it a father or mother complex.[9]

---

[8] Jung, *CW* 6 § 305.
[9] Jung, *CW* 7 § 293. For a study of images of the dead and the mourning process from the perspective of archetypal psychology, see Greg Mogenson, *Greeting the Angels: An Imaginal View of the Mourning Process* (Amityville, NY: Baywood Publishing Co., 1992).

During the same time period that Jung is writing his Fordham lectures, Freud, in Vienna, is busy completing his most significant book on the belief in ghosts and fear of the dead. In *Totem and Taboo*, Freud begins to formulate a psychological understanding of people's fear of ghosts, especially the ghosts of loved ones. Freud postulates that a person's deep feelings in relation to loved ones are basically ambivalent. Connected to every affection is some negative emotion, but often during the lifetime of the loved one the negative emotion is repressed or not acknowledged. When the loved one dies, however, the internal conflict between the positive and negative emotion becomes more acute. Rather than face the negative feelings toward the loved one internally, the individual often projects these feelings into dark places in the outer world associated with the deceased person. For Freud, fear of the dead has to do with the fundamental ambivalence of emotions in close human relations.[10]

Freud's formulation is remarkably similar to Jung's early and midlife views. In *Psychology and Alchemy*, Jung writes: "The fear of ghosts means, psychologically speaking, the overpowering of consciousness by the autonomous contents of the unconscious."[11] It is not ghosts people are afraid of, but the autonomous aspects of their own psyche.

David L. Miller, in his book *Hells & Holy Ghosts*, has compiled an extensive inventory of the many references to ghosts in the history of depth psychology, noting that so important was the role of death for Freud in the formation of the personality that he formulated a death instinct equal in significance to the role of sexuality.[12]

Following his break with Freud, Jung began to experience a period of intense psychic turmoil. During this time, Jung reports several more dreams of apparitions and records the following fantasy in which he finds himself in the "land of the dead." To facilitate the fantasy, Jung began by imagining a steep descent. Jung had the feeling during the descent that he was entering the land of the dead. There he caught sight of two figures, an old man with a white beard and a beautiful blind woman. He summoned up his courage and approached them as though they were real people, and listened attentively to what they had to

---

[10] Sigmund Freud, *Totem and Taboo: Some Points of Agreement between the Mental Lives of Savages and Neurotics* tr. J. Strachey (New York: W. W. Norton, & Co, 1950), pp. 61-63.
[11] Jung, *CW* 12 § 437n.
[12] Miller, pp. 145-155.

say. The old man explained that he was Elijah and the young woman called herself Salome. Jung would later speculate that these figures were "spirits of the dead" addressing critical questions to him that they had not been able to answer during their own lifetime.[13]

Some 15 years later, Jung was having a conversation with an Indian friend of Gandhi's and asked him about his personal guru. The man indicated his guru was the commentator on the Vedas who had died centuries before. Jung, remembering his earlier experience with Elijah, asked if he was referring to a spirit functioning as a guru? The man replied, "There are ghostly gurus too. Most people have living gurus. But there are always some who have a spirit for a teacher." Jung would later look back upon his experiences with Elijah and Salome as a kind of therapy, where he was the client and they the co-therapists, writing in his autobiography: "I was like a patient in analysis with a ghost and a woman!"[14]

The Seven Sermons to the Dead

In December of 1916, Jung had his most significant experience with apparitions, which lead to his writing *The Seven Sermons to the Dead*. He had just recorded a disturbing fantasy in which his soul had flown away. Jung regarded this event as signifying a severe disturbance in his relationship to the unconscious and expressed his concern in the following way:

> In a certain sense ... [the relationship to the soul] ... is also a relationship to the collectivity of the dead; for the unconscious corresponds to the mythic land of the dead, the land of the ancestors. If, therefore, one has a fantasy of the soul vanishing, this means that it has withdrawn into the unconscious or into the land of the dead. There it produces a mysterious animation and gives visible form to the ancestral traces.... Like a medium, it gives the dead a chance to manifest themselves. Therefore, soon after the disappearance of my soul the "dead" appeared to me, and the result was the *Septem Sermones*.[15]

---

[13] Jung, *MDR*, pp. 191-192.
[14] Jung, *MDR*, p. 186.
[15] Jung, *MDR*, p. 191.

THE LEGACY OF THE DEAD

Shortly after the fantasy of losing his soul, Jung began to experience a restlessness. An ominous atmosphere began to develop around him at home and he had a strange feeling that the air was filling with ghostly entities. It was as if his house began to be haunted. Later that night, his eldest daughter saw a white figure passing through her room. His second daughter reported that twice in the night her blanket had been pulled away, and his nine-year-old son experienced an anxiety dream. Around five o'clock the next afternoon the front doorbell began ringing repeatedly. Everyone looked to see who was there, but no one could be seen. Jung describes what happened next:

> I was sitting near the doorbell, and not only heard it but saw it moving. We all simply stared at one another. The atmosphere was thick, believe me! Then I knew that something had to happen. The whole house was filled as if there were a crowd present, crammed full of spirits. They were packed deep right up to the door, and the air was so thick it was scarcely possible to breathe. As for myself, I was all a-quiver with the question: "For God's sake, what in the world is this?" Then they cried out in a chorus, "We have come back from Jerusalem where we found not what we sought." That is the beginning of the *Septem Sermones*. Then it began to flow out of me, and in the course of three evenings the thing was written. As soon as I took up the pen, the whole ghostly assemblage evaporated. The room quieted and the atmosphere cleared. The haunting was over.[16]

From that time on, Jung reports, 'the dead' became ever more distinct, and he began referring to what he heard as "the voices of the Unanswered, Unresolved, and Unredeemed."[17] Jung felt that the questions and demands that his destiny required him to answer did not come from outside, but rather, from these encounters with the dead.

Spirits as the Exteriorization of Complexes

In 1919, in an essay entitled "The Psychological Foundation of Belief in Spirits," Jung turned his attention directly to the phenomenon of the belief in apparitions. The lecture was first delivered in England to the Society for Psychical Research and concludes with the following statement: Spirits "are, so far as my experience goes, the exteriorized effects

---

[16] Jung, *MDR*, pp. 190-191.
[17] Jung, *MDR*, pp. 191-192.

of unconscious complexes. I for one am certainly convinced that they are exteriorizations. I have repeatedly observed the telepathic effects of unconscious complexes, and also a number of parapsychic phenomena. But in all this I see no proof is forthcoming therefore I must regard this whole territory as an appendix of psychology."[18]

Jung's reduction of 'spirits of the dead' to a purely psychological explanation stands in sharp contrast to his many carefully worded statements about the existence of God. Repeatedly, Jung is careful not to reduce the existence of God to psychological predicates. Why then does he so unequivocally reduce the spirits of the dead to the exteriorized effects of unconscious complexes, when during the same period he clearly refuses to do so with respect to the existence of God? Perhaps Jung's Christian sensibility is at work in the background of his psyche. Following the lead of Protestant Reformation theology, he forecloses the realm traditionally inhabited by the spirits of the dead, reducing them, instead, to the exteriorization of unconscious complexes and parental imagoes.

Levels of Interpretation

During the years immediately following his break with Freud up through the 1920s, Jung begins to develop his own distinctive clinical hermeneutic based on two 'levels' of referentiality. The objective level of interpretation refers the psychic imago more to the perception of an objective person (the interpersonal dimension), while the subjective level shifts the focus of interpretation to the intrapsychic dynamics of the dreamer.

In the following quote we can get a sense as to how Jung subtly defines the imago in relation to the subject and object, without privileging one side over the other. He writes: "For just as the image of an object is composed subjectively on the one side, it is conditioned objectively on the other side. When I reproduce it in myself, I am producing something that is determined as much subjectively as objectively. In order to decide which side predominates in any given case, it must first be shown whether the image is reproduced for its subjective or for its objective significance. If, therefore, I dream of a person with whom I am connected by a vital interest, the interpretation

---

[18] Jung, *CW* 8 § 600.

on the objective level will certainly be nearer to the truth than the other. But if I dream of a person who is not important to me in reality, then interpretation on the subjective level will be nearer to the truth."[19]

Jung's general criterion for deciding which level of interpretation to use is the following: If the imago is of someone known personally and if that person is currently playing an active role in the dreamer's life, then the dream is to be approached on the objective level. If, however, the imago is of someone currently not playing an active role in the dreamer's life, then the subjective level is to be more emphasized.

Keeping Meaning Alive

As Jung grew older his application of these guidelines for interpretation seems to have changed, especially when he was confronted with images of the dead. In his dissertation, his early psychiatric articles, and his metapsychological papers, he tends to interpret the spirits of the dead exclusively on the subjective level, reducing them to the exteriorization of complexes. However, as he begins to approach death as a biological and psychic reality, this view seems to undergo a transformation. In 1944, at age 73, Jung had a severe illness followed by a near-fatal heart attack. Four years later, he returned to his earlier essay, "The Psychological Foundation of Belief in Spirits," and added the following curious footnote to the paper's conclusion:

> After collecting psychological experiences from many people and many countries for fifty years, I no longer feel as certain as I did in 1919, when I wrote this sentence. To put it bluntly, I doubt whether an exclusively psychological approach can do justice to the phenomena in question. Not only the findings of parapsychology, but my own theoretical reflections, outlined in 'On the Nature of the Psyche', have led me to certain postulates which touch on the realm of nuclear physics and the conception of the space-time continuum. This opens up the whole question of the transpsychic reality immediately underlying the world.[20]

---

[19] Jung, *CW* 8 § 309.
[20] Jung, *CW* 8 § 600n.

This passage reflects a significant change of mind! It is as if, during these interim years, the realm between life and death, the realm of the spirits, has begun to open up and become more experientially real. Jung can no longer explain spirits exclusively on the subjective level as exteriorized complexes. It is as if *during the process of aging* a second psychological perspective on the nature of spirits has begun to develop in Jung. Where the earlier perspective is animistic, the later is more spiritualistic.

Let us turn now to several dreams Jung reports in his autobiography that occurred during this later period in his life. *Jung's attitude towards the dead in dreams changed as he approached the reality of his own death.* He reports the following dream:

> I once had a dream in which I was attending a garden party. I saw my sister there and that greatly surprised me, for she had died some years before. A deceased friend of mine was also present. The rest were people who were still alive. Presently I saw that my sister was accompanied by a lady I knew well. Even in the dream I had drawn the conclusion that the lady was going to die. "She is already marked," I thought.[21]

Jung interprets the revenants in this dream on the literal and objective level. His deceased sister and another deceased friend in the dream are at a garden party he is attending. All the other guests are alive in outer reality. Presently Jung sees his sister accompanying a lady known to him in the past. He awakes and thinks the "lady is already marked."

A few weeks later, this woman, we are told by Jung, died. By *juxtaposing* the dream with the story of the death of the woman two weeks later, Jung seems to indicate he believes the dream should be interpreted on the *objective* level as a foreshadowing of the woman's death. Jung's own criteria, however, would seem to indicate that this dream should be understood on the *subjective* level. Neither his sister nor the marked woman was, at the time, playing a significant role in his outer life. However, by juxtaposing the dream image with the subsequent outer event, Jung focuses the meaning of the dream on the objective level. As Jung approaches the reality of his own death, and witnesses the passing away of many close friends, he begins to focus more and more

---

[21] Jung, *MDR*, p. 303.

THE LEGACY OF THE DEAD 123

on the literal and objective aspects of revenants as they appear in dreams and fantasies.

A little further in his autobiography, Jung presents another dream, again about a potential death. The dream occurred to him just before a member of his wife's family died. He writes:

> I dreamed that my wife's bed was a deep pit with stone walls. It was a grave, and somehow had a suggestion of classical antiquity about it. Then I heard a deep sigh, as if someone were giving up the ghost. A figure that resembled my wife sat up in the pit and floated upward. It wore a white gown into which curious black symbols were woven. It was three o'clock in the morning. The dream was so curious that I thought at once that it might signify a death. At seven o'clock came the news that a cousin of my wife had died at three o'clock in the morning.[22]

We are not told by Jung what the dream means. Rather, the dream-image is simply juxtaposed with the outer event, indicating that Jung believed the image was somehow related to the real-life happening. Jung's only direct comment about the dream is "that it might signify death." Rather than approaching the dream on the subjective level, he sees it as a "figurative allusion" to the death of his wife's cousin and connects the dream image to the life event metaphorically, not causally. *Through the juxtaposition of the dream image and outer event, Jung allows the metaphoric resonance between them to speak for itself.*

Later in the same chapter, entitled "On Life after Death," Jung presents another dream in which the dead appear. He writes:

> I once dreamed that I was paying a visit to a friend who had died about two weeks before. In life, this friend had never espoused anything but a conventional view of the world, and had remained stuck in this unreflecting attitude. In the dream ... [m]y friend sat at a table with his daughter, who had studied psychology in Zurich. I knew that she was telling him about psychology. He was so fascinated by what she was saying that he greeted me only with a casual wave of the hand, as though to intimate: 'Don't disturb me.' The greeting was at the same time a dismissal.[23]

---

[22] Jung, *MDR*, p. 303.
[23] Jung, *MDR*, p. 309.

Jung's interpretation of this dream is again quite striking. He writes, "The dream told me that now, in a manner which of course remains incomprehensible to me, he was required to grasp the reality of his psychic existence, which he had never been capable of doing during his life."[24]

Individuation after Death

Jung interprets the dream as referring to the process of psychologically educating his friend's soul. Notice, it is his dead friend who Jung believes is required to "grasp the reality of his psychic existence," something the friend did not do during the course of his life. An interpretation of his dream on the subjective level might have viewed it as the process of Jung's anima, the neighbor's daughter in the dream, psychologizing conventional man's experience of death. Jung, however, does not emphasize this dimension of his dream. What Jung focuses on, instead, is a new idea developing in his psyche concerning the *soul's continuing to evolve even after the death of the body. The soul of the deceased attempts to attain in death the awareness it fails to achieve in life.*

This idea is further developed a little later in the chapter when Jung presents another dream in which his deceased wife appears. He writes, "... [A]bout a year after my wife's death—I suddenly awoke one night and knew that I had been with her in the south of France, in Provence, and had spent an entire day with her. She was engaged in studies of the Grail there. That seemed significant to me, for she had died before completing her work on this subject."[25]

The dream is very simple, but profoundly moving. It takes place a year after his wife's death. In the dream, Jung is with Emma in the south of France, where she has been studying the Grail legends. His approach to this dream is instructive. Jung first attempts an interpretation on the subjective level, but rejects it because he already knows that meaning. He then tries an interpretation on the objective level. The process is described in the following passage: "Interpretation on the subjective level—that my anima had not yet finished with the work she had to do—yielded nothing of interest; I know quite well that I am not yet finished with that. But the thought that my wife was continuing after death to work on her

---

[24] Jung, *MDR*, p. 309.
[25] Jung, *MDR*, p. 309.

further spiritual development—however that may be conceived—struck me as meaningful and held a measure of reassurance for me."[26]

This passage makes two important points. First, the criterion Jung uses to establish which level to interpret the dream on is now "meaningfulness," not recent personal involvement, nor truthfulness, nor even correctness. The second point has to do with his idea that *Emma's soul continues to evolve even after her death*. He does not elaborate further on this idea, other than to note that the thought provided him with "a measure of reassurance."

One cannot help but be moved by the authenticity of Jung's comments about these dreams. 'Spirits of the dead' seem to affect Jung so deeply as he ages that repeatedly in interpreting them he goes against his basic principles of dream interpretation. What might be going on here?

Jung provides us with something of an answer a little further on in the chapter. He makes the following comment about dream interpretation in general: "... [I]t is so important not to have any preconceived, doctrinaire opinions about the statements made by dreams. As soon as a certain 'monotony of interpretation' strikes us, we know that our approach has become doctrinaire and hence sterile."[27]

Is it possible that Jung's resistance to interpreting these dreams on the subjective level has to do with the fact that this approach had become tired, worn out, and monotonous, full of doctrinaire ideas? For example, instead of approaching the dream as referring to his "anima development," a preconceived notion associated with the subjective level of interpretation, he takes a different approach. By shifting his focus back to the objective level, he is able to *keep the meaningfulness of the dream alive*. Consider for a moment the following passage from the same chapter. Jung is confronted by a fantasy image of a deceased friend. Notice how Jung's narrative construction works with the tension between the objective and subjective dimensions in this waking fantasy.

> One night I lay awake thinking of the sudden death of a friend whose funeral had taken place the day before. I was deeply concerned. Suddenly I felt that he was in the room. It seemed to me that he stood at the foot of my bed and was asking me to go with him. I did not have the feeling of an apparition; rather, it was an inner visual image of him, which I explained to myself as a

---

[26] Jung, *MDR*, p. 309.
[27] Jung, *MDR*, p. 312.

fantasy. But in all honesty I had to ask myself, "Do I have any proof that this is a fantasy? Suppose it is not a fantasy, suppose my friend is really here and I decided he was only a fantasy—would that not be abominable of me?" Yet I had equally little proof that he stood before me as an apparition. Then I said to myself, "Proof is neither here nor there! Instead of explaining him away as a fantasy, I might just as well give him the benefit of the doubt and for experiment's sake credit him with reality." The moment I had that thought, he went to the door and beckoned me to follow him. So I was going to have to play along with him! That was something I hadn't bargained for. I had to repeat my argument to myself once more. *Only then did I follow him in my imagination* [emphasis added].[28]

In his imagination, Jung is led out of his house through the garden and down the road to his friend's home, in reality located several hundred yards away. Jung enters the house and his friend takes him into his study.

> He climbed on a stool and showed me the second of five books with red bindings which stood on the second shelf from the top. Then the vision broke off. I was not acquainted with his library and did not know what books he owned. Certainly I could never have made out from below the title of the books he had pointed out to me on the second shelf from the top.
>
> This experience seemed to me so curious that the next morning I went to his widow and asked whether I could look up something in my friend's library. Sure enough, there was a stool standing by the bookcase I had seen in my vision, and even before I came closer I could see the five books with red bindings. I stepped up on the stool so as to be able to read the titles. They were translations of the novels of Emile Zola. The title of the second volume read: *The Legacy of the Dead.* The contents seemed to me of no interest. Only the title was extremely significant with the experience.[29]

This story is quite remarkable in the way Jung plays with and is caught up in the tension between the intrapsychic and the interpersonal, the imaginal and the real. The composition is like a Moebius strip. In

---

[28] Jung, *MDR*, p. 312.
[29] Jung, *MDR*, pp. 312-313.

THE LEGACY OF THE DEAD

the first part of the story, we are on one side, the subjective level, but by the second half of the story the reader has been seamlessly moved to the other side, to the objective level.

Jung restricts his interpretation of the story to a single comment, noting, "Only the title was extremely significant with the experience." *He simply juxtaposes the title, "The Legacy of the Dead," with the experience and lets the reader's imagination fill in the rest of the interpretation.*

Locating Interpretation in Lived Time

The paradoxical phenomenon of multiple interpretations of a single event is not limited to the world of psychology. In physics, for example, the analysis of light has two different interpretations, one explained from the standpoint of particles, and the other from the perspective of waves. Both explanations are valid, and yet, they are in a certain sense mutually exclusive. The observer is free to conduct experiments according to either assumption, but the experimenter must realize that in choosing one interpretation he excludes, momentarily, the other. What is most important, however, is the standpoint of the observer who is always located in lived time. *As we age, our sense of time changes, and that change influences our clinical hermeneutic. What we view metaphorically at one point in the human life cycle, may appear increasingly literal at another moment. Our therapeutic hermeneutic is always embedded in our experience of time*, and rarely, if ever, is the significance of lived time factored into our understanding of clinical interpretation.

In the course of Jung's life, he was confronted by 'spirits of the dead' in many different forms, ranging from personal dreams of his deceased parents, to theoretical tropes in his metapsychology, to dreams and fantasy images of departed loved ones and deceased friends near the end of his life. During the process of aging, *the quality of Jung's sense of time changed, and that transformation exerted a significant influence on his understanding of the role of the dead in psychic life.*

CHAPTER SEVEN

Psyche, Language, and Biology

> [T]he major structural and functional innovations that make human brains capable of unprecedented mental feats evolved in response to the use of something as abstract and virtual as the power of words. ... [T]he first use of symbolic reference by some distant ancestors changed how natural selection processes have affected hominid brain evolution ever since.[1]
> —Terrence W. Deacon

In our final chapter, we will take up the question of human evolution and weave it together with various themes developed earlier: the psychic function of productive and reproductive imagining, originary principles, interpretation, the acquisition of language, and temporality. All these themes come together when we attempt to formulate a depth psychological understanding of how the psyche relates to biology, culture, and language. This is no small task. Each one of these complex areas of study is a challenge. Formulating how they interact over time in the development of human nature is even more challenging. We will explore the evolutionary process through which structural components of the human psyche emerge out of the interaction of biology with language and culture.[2]

In recent years, the very notion of human nature and its 'essential' or archetypal aspects has become the focus of an intense debate between two competing theoretical perspectives.[3] On one side of the debate are the social constructivists who focus on the role played by language and

---

[1] Terrence W. Deacon, *The Symbolic Species: The Co-Evolution of Language and the Brain* (New York: W. W. Norton & Co., 1997), p. 322.
[2] George Hogenson, "The Baldwin Effect: A Neglected Influence on C. G. Jung's Evolutionary Thinking," *The Journal of Analytical Psychology* 46.4 (2001): 591-611. (Originally, "Evolution, Psychology and the Emergence of the Psyche," a paper delivered at The National Conference of Jungian Analysts, Santa Fe, New Mexico, Oct. 18, 1999.)
[3] Steven Pinker, *The Blank Slate: The Modern Denial of Human Nature* (New York: Viking Press, 2002). See also, Joseph Carroll, *Evolution and Literary Theory* (Columbia, MO: University of Missouri Press, 1995).

culture in 'constructing' our sense of reality, as well as the archetypal aspects of the human psyche. On the other side of the debate, the evolutionary psychologists emphasize the role of evolution and human biology. The function and ontological status of the archetype differs significantly in each perspective. Social constructivists view 'the archetype' as a linguistic construct, a metaphoric by-product of language or a cultural artifact, while evolutionary psychologists construe archetypes as genetically determined entities, rooted in biology and driven by the evolutionary process. To understand the importance of this controversy more clearly, we will begin with a review of key elements in this language/biology debate and attempt in the process to formulate a new understanding of *how language and culture interact with biology in the natural history of the human psyche.*

Postmodernism and Social Constructivism

During the past twenty years, a revolution in thought has taken place in the social sciences. This has variously been referred to as the language turn in philosophy, postmodernism in the arts, and constructivism in the social sciences. The common element in all these movements has been an intense focus on the roles language and culture play in the construction of our theories as well as our identities.[4]

The language turn in philosophy has led to the realization that theory of any kind, be it literary, philosophical, clinical, or scientific, does not allow for a transparent view to the so-called empirical world. Our theories and their explanatory terms (for example, archetype, drive, self) have no location outside of language, neither objective nor empirical, and can never be a ground, only a mediator. The reader of any *text*—fictional or scientific—is suspended between the literal and metaphoric

---

[4] See Ludwig Wittgenstein, *Philosophical Investigations,* tr. G. E. M. Anscombe (New York: Macmillan Company,1958); Jacques Derrida, *Of Grammatology,* tr. G. C. Spivak (Baltimore: The Johns Hopkins University Press, 1974); David Theo Goldberg, ed., *Multiculturalism: A Critical Reader* (Oxford: Blackwell Publishers Ltd., 1994); Michel Foucault, *Madness and Civilization: A History of Insanity in the Age of Reason,* tr. R. Howard (London: Tavistock, 1967); Michael Adams, *The Multicultural Imagination* (London: Routledge, 1996); Christopher Hauke, *Jung and the Postmodern: The Interpretation of Realities* (London: Routledge, 2000); Paul Kugler, "The Unconscious in a Postmodern Depth Psychology," *C. G. Jung and the Humanities,* eds. K. Barnaby & P. Acierno (Princeton, NJ: Princeton University Press, 1990); Paul Kugler, "Clinical Authority: Some Thoughts out of Season," *Quadrant: The Journal of Contemporary Jungian Thought* 23.2 (1990): 81-85; Judith Teicholz, *Kohut, Loewald, and the Postmoderns: A Comparative Study of Self and Relationship* (Hillsdale, NJ: The Analytic Press, 1999).

significances of the text's 'root' metaphors, unable to maintain a fixed connection between the various meanings of the root metaphor and a single unambiguous referent. This inevitably leads to a *linguistic relativity* and a *semantic indeterminacy* with respect to any textual formulation.

Our theories and descriptions of personality are not only influenced by the linguistic medium we use, but also subject to our 'personal equation.' Social constructivists emphasize not only the language-locked features of theory, but also the enormous diversity of psychological phenomena found in cultures around the world and throughout history. Cultural differences are explained in terms of *differences* in local conditions, linguistic constraints, and history. From this perspective, it is not the world, nor its properties that are constructed, but rather, *the vocabularies in whose terms we know them.* The vocabularies (scientific, mathematical, rational, psychological, mythological, fictional, etc.) used to describe the world and its properties are constructed by human beings living in a specific geographical place, at a particular moment in history, embedded in a cultural context, speaking one of many possible languages, at a certain age in their human life cycle. All these factors produce subtle effects on our *descriptions of the world*. As any one of these factors shifts, our understanding of the properties shifts as well.

For a better appreciation of the important role language plays in structuring the psyche, let us turn for a moment to the ontogenetic implications of language acquisition in psychic development.

The Birth of the Mimetic Function

In the psychological life of a child, few events have greater significance than the acquisition of language. The development of the capacity for psychic representation occurs in the infant between six and eighteen months. During this time, the child develops the capacity to separate from and recognize its own image as other. For example, an infant who has previously shown no signs of recognition when looking in a mirror suddenly begins to smile on seeing its reflected image, for the child has developed the capacity to recognize its own representation.[5] The achievement of this originary reflexivity differentiates the psychic image

---

[5] Jacques Lacan, *Ecrits,* tr. A. Sheridan (New York: W. W. Norton & Co., 1977); Paul Kugler, "Jacques Lacan: Post-Modern Depth Psychology and the Birth of the Self-Reflexive Subject," *The Book of the Self: Person, Pretext, and Process,* eds. P. Eisendrath & J. Hall (New York: New York University Press, 1987).

of the child from its physical body. Prior to this stage, the child lacks the capacity to distinguish the representational from the biological. But during the mirror stage, this unity of experience is split and *the child acquires the capacity to differentiate the psychic image from biological experience.*

Through the process of developing the capacity for representation and replication, first on the level of psychic images and later on the level of language proper, a self becomes divided from itself and in the process capable of self-reflection. The importance of the creation of a divided subject, an ego/self structure capable of self-reflection, cannot be overemphasized.[6] For in acquiring linguistic competence, the infant learns to speak to the world through a network of collectively determined symbols.[7]

From Imago to Word: An Ontological Rupture

The differentiation between the biological infant and the psychic image with which the infant identifies is only the anticipation of a far more profound differentiation of the psyche that occurs during language acquisition. Through the acquisition of language, the mirror image of the body is replaced with a linguistic image, the first-person pronoun. With the acquisition of language comes a second ontological rupture, this time between word and body, between description and event. During the mirror stage, the human subject becomes possible when neurological development allows the infant to distinguish objects, and the human subject becomes actual when the child develops the mimetic capacity for representation and replication. Let us turn now to the phylogenetic significance of language development in the evolution of the psyche, and in particular, to Darwin and the recent advances in evolutionary psychology.

The Darwinian Revival

The current revival of interest in Darwin can be traced back to the early 1960s when William Hamilton, a rather shy postgraduate student at the London School of Economics, began to question Darwin's theory of group selection. If altruism benefits the species or the group in which a person lives, it would be favored, Darwin argued, by natural selection.

---

[6] Paul Kugler, "The 'Subject' of Dreams," *Dreaming: Journal of the Association for the Study of Dreams* 3.2 (1993): 123-136.
[7] Lacan, *Ecrits*; Paul Kugler, *The Alchemy of Discourse: Image, Sound and Psyche*, rev. ed. (Zürich: Daimon Verlag, 2002).

Groups in which people sacrifice themselves for the common good would be more cohesive and, therefore, more successful than other groups. Darwin's theory of group selection had remained largely unquestioned until the 1960s. Hamilton argued that within any group, altruists would tend to be exploited by non-altruists, who would then end up with the majority of the resources. This in turn should make the non-altruists better able to reproduce and survive longer. Eventually, he argued, the altruists would become extinct. If this is the case, Hamilton wondered, *how could the genes responsible for altruistic behavior survive and be passed down from generation to generation?*

As a child, Hamilton had often helped his mother with the honeybees she kept in hives near their home. While struggling to understand Darwin's theory of group selection, he remembered being stung as a child when he would go too near a hive. Worker bees would sense possible danger, fly out, and sting the intruder. A barb on the end of the bee's stinger would lodge in the intruders flesh, and as the bee tried to fly away, it would die tearing off the back portion of its body. A successful sting by a worker bee protecting the colony meant certain death. Hamilton wondered how Darwinian evolution could possibly account for such a suicidal form of adaptation, especially when none of the sacrificial worker bee's genes were transmitted to subsequent generations?

Adopting the Gene's Perspective

Hamilton explained the lethal altruistic behavior in terms of the bee's reproductive system. Worker bees do not mate, leaving all reproduction to the queen and the drones. What Hamilton realized, however, was that all the worker bees come from the same queen and therefore share the same percentage of her genes. Hamilton theorized that from the point of view of the genes, it did not matter if an individual organism lived or died, but only that a copy of the genes was passed on. In the case of the worker bee that stung him, copies of the same genes continued to live in all the other bees in the hive. By shifting the evolutionary perspective from a focus on an individual organism to the gene itself, Hamilton was able to formulate his notion of 'inclusive fitness' or 'kin selection,' arguing that *what is of prime importance in evolution is the survival of the genes, not the individual.*[8] This shift in perspective from the individual

---

[8] William D. Hamilton, "The Evolution of Altruistic Behavior," *American Naturalist* 97 (1963): 354-56.

organism to the gene reoriented evolutionary theory and set the stage for the modern revival of interest in Darwin's theories.

One of the most influential books in the Neo-Darwinian movement is Richard Dawkins' *The Selfish Gene* (1976). The main theme of this book is drawn from Hamilton's idea that the gene is selfish, more concerned with its own survival than with that of the individual who carries it. Dawkins' book was controversial at the time, since it propounded the idea that humans are "survival machines," "robot vehicles blindly programmed to preserve the selfish molecules known as genes" (Preface to *The Selfish Gene*). When Dawkins' selfish gene theory was first put forward over twenty-five years ago as a modern upgrade of Darwin's natural selection, it was considered radical. Today, in the field of evolutionary psychology, the idea that genes will do anything necessary to reproduce themselves in the next generation has become orthodoxy in many quarters.[9] These neo-Darwinians insist that underneath all the broad cultural variations, the essential structure of human minds is identical.

For many of the new Darwinians, the most significant evolution of the human brain took place prior to the invention of agriculture during the Neolithic period.[10] On the genetic level, evolutionary change is very slow. It has been only 10,000 years since the Neolithic revolution, when humans first began growing their own food and building cities. From the perspective of evolutionary psychology, not enough time has elapsed since the Pleistocene period for human behavior to have produced a change on the genetic level. Consequently, the minds of contemporary humans must reflect structural adaptations evolved to meet the

---

[9] "Evolutionary Psychology" as used here refers to a particular approach to evolution championed by John Tooby, an anthropologist, and his wife, Leda Cosmides, a psychologist. Together they run the Center for Evolutionary Psychology at the University of California at Santa Barbara. See Richard Dawkins, *The Selfish Gene* (Oxford: Oxford University Press, 1976); John Tooby & Leda Cosmides, "On the Universality of Human Nature and the Uniqueness of the Individual: The Role of Genetics and Adaptation," *Journal of Personality* 58.1 (1990): 17-67; John Tooby & Leda Cosmides, "The Past Explains the Present: Emotional Adaptations and the Structure of Ancestral Environments," *Ethology and Sociobiology* 11 (1990): 375-424; Daniel C. Dennett, *Darwin's Dangerous Idea: Evolution and the Meanings of Life* (New York: Simon & Schuster, 1995).

[10] Tooby & Cosmides, "The Past Explains the Present"; Steven Pinker, *The Language Instinct* (New York: HarperCollins, 1994); Steven Pinker, *How the Mind Works* (New York: W. W. Norton, 1997); Anthony Stevens & John Price, *Evolutionary Psychiatry: A New Beginning* (London: Routledge, 1996); Anthony Stevens, *Ariadne's Clue: A Guide to the Symbols of Humankind* (Princeton, NJ: Princeton University Press, 1999).

challenges faced by our hunter-gatherer ancestors. To understand a person's current mental behavior, including his or her psychopathology, the clinician needs, in part, to understand the behavior in terms of adaptations evolved to meet the challenges of the Pleistocene environment.[11] Anthony Stevens and John Price in their book *Evolutionary Psychiatry* theorize that the archetypal structures of today's psyche are adapted to the environment of the Pleistocene period and have evolved through the process of adaptation and natural selection. Their theory is predicated on several assumptions: (1) the process of evolution is the same for all species, (2) learning, language, culture and consciousness play only secondary roles in the evolutionary equation, and (3) archetypes are embedded in the genetic code of human biology. But what if human evolution is fundamentally different from the biologically driven process found in other species? Is it possible that in acquiring the capacity for symbolic representation our species crossed the animal/human divide and *forever altered its evolutionary process*?

Biology and Language: A Co-evolutionary Process

In recent years, an alternative to Darwinian evolution has begun to take shape. Rather than focusing on the biological similarities in evolution between humans and other species, this approach emphasizes, instead, *what makes human evolution different—the role of language and culture in the evolutionary process.*[12]

The great evolutionary leap forward for humans came with the development of symbolic representation and language. While certain other species have evolved a limited ability to communicate (for example, chimpanzees, parrots, dolphins), the difference between human language, with its *capacity for symbolism*, and all other natural modes of communicating is great.[13] But, why, we might ask, is the development of language and its capacity for symbolic representation so important from an evolutionary point of view? Where the gene replicates biological information and passes it on physically to the next generation, *language allows for the production and reproduction of a new kind of information*, psychic

---

[11] Anthony Stevens, *Archetypes: A Natural History of the Self* (New York: Quill Books, 1983).
[12] Deacon; William Durham, *Coevolution: Genes, Culture and Human Diversity* (Stanford, CA: Stanford University Press, 1991); Susan Blackmore, *The Meme Machine* (Oxford: Oxford University Press, 1999); Hogenson; Steven Mithen, *The Prehistory of the Mind* (London: Thames & Hudson, 1996).
[13] Deacon, pp. 254-278.

and cultural information, which can also be duplicated and passed on to other members of the species. The development of this productive and mimetic capacity constitutes the emergence in human evolution of a second means for transmitting information across generations. Prior to the capacity for human language, it was not possible to reproduce learning on a symbolic level. However, as soon as language developed, so too did the ability to disseminate the products of learning.

How might this cultural and linguistic process of disseminating intergenerational information dynamically interact with the process of genetic evolution? Consider, for a moment, the dramatic increase in the average height of humans over the past two centuries. How much of this change in human biology can be attributed to genetic transformations in our species? According to Daniel Dennett, a staunch Darwinian, little if any at all, can be accounted for through changes in the biological evolution of human genetics.[14] During the period in which the dramatic growth change has occurred, only about ten generations have elapsed. Even if there were significant evolutionary forces in the natural environment supporting such an adaptive change, the time frame in genetic terms is far too small to account for such a dramatic change in physical stature. What has changed significantly, however, during this same time period has been human living conditions, medical care, public health practices, farming techniques, and dietary habits. These *cultural innovations produced significant alterations in the human phenotype* over the past two hundred years.

So moved is Dennett by the power of cultural innovation in the evolutionary process, that he concedes:

> Anyone who worries about 'genetic determinism' should be reminded that virtually all the differences discernible between the people of, say, Plato's day and the people living today—their physical talents, proclivities, attitudes, prospects—must be due to cultural changes, since fewer than two hundred generations separate us from Plato. Environmental changes due to cultural innovations change the landscape of phenotypic expression so much, and so fast, however, that they can in principle change the

---

[14] Dennett, pp. 335-342.

genetic selection pressures rapidly—the Baldwin Effect is a simple instance of such a change in selection pressure due to widespread behavioral innovation.[15]

The Baldwin Effect

The Baldwin Effect is named after one of its discoverers, James Baldwin, a leading nineteenth-century American child psychologist. The Baldwin Effect was simultaneously discovered by two other nineteenth-century evolutionists, Conway L. Morgan and H. F. Osborn.[16] An early proponent of evolution, Baldwin was concerned about an evolutionary theory that left mind out of the equation. He proceeded to demonstrate that humans could alter or guide the *further evolution of their species by solving environmental problems during their lifetime, thereby making these problems easier to solve in the future and altering the conditions of competition for their offspring.*

Baldwin's theory is contained in his essay, "A New Factor in Evolution," in which he concludes: "Evolution is, therefore, not more biological than psychological."[17] The 'Baldwin Effect' is an important contribution to evolutionary theory, introducing mind and psychology into the evolutionary process without falling victim to the problems that plagued Lamarck and his theory of direct intergenerational transmission of acquired characteristics.

George Hogenson, a Jungian analyst and philosopher, has written a seminal essay on "Evolution, Psychology and the Emergence of the Psyche" in which he documents the influence of Baldwin and Morgan on Jung's theory of archetypes. Through a carefully researched analysis of the sources Jung draws on in his early formulation of the relation between archetype and instinct, Hogenson convincingly demonstrates the influence of Baldwin and Morgan on Jung's theory. Where Freud was clearly a Lamarckian, Jung did not subscribe to the theory of direct intergenerational transmission of acquired characteristics. Instead,

---

[15] Dennett, p. 338.
[16] For more information on the significance of James Baldwin in the history of evolutionary theory see Hogenson's "The Baldwin Effect." See also, Robert J. Richards, *Darwin and the Emergence of Evolutionary Theories of Mind* (Chicago: University of Chicago Press, 1987), especially pp. 480-503.
[17] James Mark Baldwin, "A New Factor in Evolution," *Adaptive Individuals in Evolving Populations: Models and Algorithms* eds. R. K. Belew & M. Mitchell (Reading, MA: Addison-Wesley, 1996), pp. 59-80. See also, Hogenson, "The Baldwin Effect."

Jung was influenced by the work of Baldwin and Morgan to understand the role played by psychology and learning in human evolution.[18]

Hogenson integrates Baldwin's early theoretical work with current advances in cognitive psychology and the neurosciences. Since the early 1980s, the development of powerful new computers has created a revolution in our ability to research certain evolutionary questions. Researchers are now able to simulate with computers complex evolutionary processes that in nature would require far too much time to complete in a laboratory setting. In 1987, Geoffrey Hinton and Steven Nowlan published a ground-breaking paper describing the use of computer simulation to research how learning effects human evolution. Hinton and Nowlan demonstrated that if an organism could set some of its genetic variables through a learning factor, it adapted better than did organisms that rely entirely on random variation and natural selection. Hinton and Nowlan's computer experiment and many subsequent variations on it, further demonstrate that *language and cultural innovation have become such powerful forces in evolution that they are now capable of modifying many of the earlier genetically driven processes of biological transformation.*[19]

Imitation and the Process of Replication

Susan Blackmore, a British psychologist, has developed a new theory of evolution based on folding Baldwin's insights back into a more traditional Darwinian framework. Blackmore's theory builds upon Dawkins' earlier concept of the meme, the cultural equivalent of the gene.[20] A 'meme' is the smallest unit of cultural information capable of being replicated and passed on to subsequent generations according to the laws of natural selection and survival of the fittest. The development of the capacity for imitation, according to Blackmore, sets our ancestors apart from all other species. Once imitation has developed, a second, much faster means for disseminating information enters the evolutionary process. The replication and transmission of memes between humans

---

[18] Hogenson's research challenges the claim by Anthony Stevens that Jung was influenced by Lamarck. See Stevens, *Archetypes*, pp. 12-18.
[19] Edwin Hutchins & Brian Hazelhurst, "Learning in the Cultural Process," *Artifical Life II: Proceedings of the Workshop on the Synthesis and Simulation of Living Systems, Santa Fe, 1990*, eds. C. G. Langton, C. Taylor, J. D. Farmer, & S. Rasmussen (Redwood City, CA: Addison-Wesley, 1992), pp. 689-706; Horst Hendricks-Jansen, *Catching Ourselves in the Act: Situated Activity, Interactive Emergence, Evolutiuon, and Human Thought* (Cambridge, MA: MIT Press, 1996); Hogenson; Pinker, *How the Mind Works*.
[20] Blackmore; Dawkins, *Selfish Gene*.

changes the environment in which genes are selected and, in doing so, forces them to build better and better meme-spreading apparatuses. The primary function of language, according to Blackmore, is the spreading of memes, which results in the dramatic altering of biological evolution.

Blackmore's application of Darwin's natural selection to cover any kind of replication in which copies are made and transmitted to other members of the species presents certain problems. For example, psychologists know only too well that we unconsciously imitate others, especially our parents, and through this process transmit certain patterns of behavior from one generation to the next. For Blackmore, the capacity to unconsciously imitate and pass on discrete elements of information to other members of the species is the key factor in human evolution. While I would agree that the ability to reproduce psychic and cultural information is critical in the development of the child ontogenetically, as well as the species phylogenetically, I question the assumption that the same genetic process of biological replication is being 'duplicated' on the psychic and cultural levels. Evolutionary geneticists have known for many years that natural selection works only if there is a low rate of mutation. For Blackmore to apply Darwin's laws of natural selection to the cultural and psychological realms the *duplication of memes must have a high degree of fidelity*, i.e., the quality of the copying and transmission must be extremely good. Just here arises the problem: memes appear to have a low degree of fidelity. When memes are transmitted, there is considerably more 'noise' (mutation) than is found in the process of genetic transmission. Consider for a moment the process by which the child imitates and introjects the parent. *The child's psychic image of the parent (a meme, in Blackmore's theory) is not an exact replication of the actual parent.* It was precisely this low fidelity that prompted depth psychologists to use the term psychic imago, rather than representation. For Blackmore to apply Darwin's theory of natural selection and survival of the fittest to memes successfully, she must subscribe to the assumption that psychic and cultural images (memes) are high-fidelity copies. I would propose, instead, that the low fidelity encountered in the transmission of psychic and cultural information reflects the presence of *productive as well as reproductive processes*. Human creativity enters this second, non-biological, line of intergenerational transmission *in the difference between the original and the reproduction.*[21]

---

[21] For a review of this problem in the history of Western thought, see chapter one of this book.

The Emergent Properties of Archetypes

Language acquisition with its capacity to produce and reproduce information is an essential factor in the evolution of modern humans. Our evolution differs from other species in its dependence on not one, but two, lines of transmission of species-specific information. Once the capacity for symbolic representation develops, first through images, and then through words, a new means for disseminating intergenerational information is introduced into the evolutionary process. Hogenson theorizes that *archetypes are properties that have emerged out of the dynamic relationship between biology and language.* This is a bold and important claim that attempts to account for the emergence of archetypal properties out of the dynamic relationship between human biology and the newly evolved capacity for symbolic representation. In 1989, Lionel Corbett and I adopted a similar position in the context of a discussion of "The Origin and Evolution of the Self."[22] There we addressed the significance of explaining *the emergent properties of the self* without appealing to structuring principles outside the system (personality) itself, for example, using biology to explain psychology. In physiologically based psychology, there has been a tradition of looking for 'smart' microscopic cells to explain macroscopic psychological events. This approach has always had its problems. The model inevitably regresses to either genetics or the physical environment without ever accounting for the structurality of the microscopic cells (e.g. the structurality of the genetic code). Psychology's theoretical challenge is to explain how macroscopic psychic regularities emerge out of microscopic physiological elements, such that *the psychological regularities exhibit a certain degree of autonomy.* The regularities of personality form the basis for the laws of psychology, just as biological regularities form the basis for the laws of physiology, and physical regularities form the basis for the laws of physics.

The regularity of archetypes at the psychological level has its own unique lawfulness.[23] As we scale up from physics to biology to psychology, each successive level of complexity is sustained by regularities that are manifest on the level below. For example, in physics the

---

[22] Lionel Corbett & Paul Kugler, "The Self in Jung and Kohut," *Dimensions of Self Experience*, ed. A. Goldberg (Hillsdale, NJ: The Analytic Press, 1989).

[23] Whereas rules run into the problem of representationalism and the regress problem of embodiment, laws avoid this dilemma.

regularities of subatomic particles as described by quantum electrodynamics form important boundary conditions for the behavior that *emerges* as we scale up to the atomic level. At this level, the behavior of electrons is influenced by the structural properties, the boundary conditions, provided by the subatomic particles. However, and this is the important point, the behavior of electrons is not explainable, nor reducible to, the structural properties of the lower level. At the atomic level, a new set of regularities appears, describable by its own set of laws, Schrödinger's Wave Mechanics or Heisenberg's Matrix Mechanics. Beyond the atomic level, regularities describable by the laws of Classical Mechanics begin to emerge. At each level, the scale below provides a stable set of constraints, or 'boundary conditions,' for the dynamics on the next higher level. As we scale up through the biological and psychological levels, the regularities that emerge are similarly influenced by the more micro scales, but are not reducible to them.[24] My theoretical understanding of archetypes is congruent with Hogenson's position that archetypes are not located in the genetic structure of human biology,[25] but rather are *properties that have emerged out of the dynamic relationship between biology and language.*

Crossing the Animal/Human Divide

Our theories of evolution have come a long way since Darwin's early biologically driven model based on variation and natural selection. Whereas other species evolve along biological lines, humans develop through a co-evolutionary spiral involving biology, language and culture. Cultural artifacts and human language have been around for only a brief period of time in biological terms, and yet, our species has used its newly acquired symbolic ability to transform our planet, as well as our biology. The development of the capacity for *imaging forever altered human evolution, transforming the process into an interactive dynamic between the forces of biology and symbolic representation: sexuality and image.*[26]

---

[24] Michael T. Turvey & Peter N. Kugler, *Information, Natural Law, and the Self-Assembly of Rhythmic Movement* (Hillsdale, NJ: Erlbaum Associates, 1987).
[25] Stevens, *Ariadne's Clue.*
[26] "Perhaps it was the step from constrained virtual reality, where the brain simulates a model of what the sense organs are telling it, to unconstrained virtual reality, in which the brain simulates things that are not actually there at the time—imagination, daydreaming, 'what if?' calculations about hypothetical futures. ... We can get outside the universe. I mean in the sense of putting a model inside our skulls." Richard Dawkins, *Unweaving the Rainbow* (Boston: Mariner Books, 1998), pp. 311-312.

A Retrospective

We began this book with several questions: What role does imaging play in personality formation, psychopathology, and the onset of human subjectivity? How are psychic images, dreams, and their interpretation related to 'the unconscious' and the act of self-reflection? In the process of exploring these questions, many 'figures' have been evoked: Freud, Jung, Nietzsche, and Darwin; the Subject, Seduction, Revenants, and Evolution. Long after the departure of these 'figures,' there remains in consciousness a haunting awareness that it is not possible to 'see through' their ghostly images clearly to a reality that is metaphysical, historical, or psychobiographical. These 'spirits of the letter' are not transparent to the world, but actively 'figure' in the creation of our subject. Through the process of reading, we identify with a 'figure of speech,' taking it literally, as does the post-mirror-stage child in that inaugural first reading. As various other figures begin to appear and disappear in our gaze, this process of identifying and dis-identifying brings into being both the subject of this text, as well as our own subjectivity. Through this mirroring, 'interpreting' the figure first on the 'objective level,' then on the 'subjective level,' we find the subject continually shifting sites, changing identity. This reflexivity renders a definitive reading impossible, for we are always suspended somewhere between the literal and the figural, thrown into the semantic indeterminacy of the text. The figures are suspended in the site of reflexivity, somewhere between the called and the so-called. And somewhere in the intermixing of the figures in this text with those in our subjectivity, a significance begins to emerge, always seeming to allude to something behind, beyond the text, to an elsewhere, to a truth that this text itself does not quite yield.

Bibliography

Abrams, Meyer H. *The Mirror and the Lamp: Romantic Theory and the Critical Tradition.* Oxford: Oxford University Press, 1971.
Adams, Michael. *The Fantasy Principle: Psychoanalysis of the Imagination.* Hove, UK: Brunner-Routledge, 2004.
——. *The Multicultural Imagination.* London: Routledge, 1996.
Adler, Gerald & Dan H. Buie. "Aloneness and Borderline Psychopathology: Developmental Issues." *International Journal of Psychoanalysis* 60 (1979): 83-96.
Aristotle. *De Anima.* Tr. H. Lawson-Tangred. Harmondsworth, UK: Penguin Classics, 1987.
——. *Metaphysics.* Tr. R. Hope. Ann Arbor: The University of Michigan Press, 1952.
Avens, Robert. *Imagination is Reality.* Dallas: Spring Publications, 1980.
Baldwin, James Mark. "A New Factor in Evolution." *Adaptive Individuals in Evolving Populations: Models and Algorithms.* Eds. R. K. Belew & M. Mitchell. Reading, MA: Addison-Wesley, 1996.
Barthes, Roland. *The Pleasure of the Text.* Tr. R. Howard. London: Macmillan & Co., 1976.
Benjamin, Jessica. *Shadow of the Other: Intersubjectivity and Gender in Psychoanalysis.* London: Routledge, 1998.
Bion, Wilfred R. *Learning from Experience.* London: William Heinemann, 1962.
——. "A Theory of Thinking, Part II of the Psycho-analytic Study of Thinking." *International Journal of Psychoanalysis* 43.2 (1962): 306-10.
Blackmore, S. *The Meme Machine.* Oxford: Oxford University Press, 1999.
Block, Ned, ed. *Imagery.* Cambridge, MA: MIT Press, 1982.
Bollas, Christopher. *Forces of Destiny: Psychoanalysis and Human Idiom.* London: Free Association Books, 1989.
Browne, Angela & David Finkelhor. "Impact of Child Sexual Abuse: A Review of the Research." *Psychological Bulletin* 99.1 (1986).
Bundy, M.W. *The Theory of Imagination in Classical and Medieval Thought.* University of Illinois Studies in Language and Literature, Vol. XII. Urbana, IL: University of Illinois Press, 1927.
Carroll, Joseph. *Evolution and Literary Theory.* Columbia, MO: University of Missouri Press, 1995.
Casey, Edward S. *Imagining: A Phenomenological Study.* Bloomington, IN: Indiana University Press, 1976.
Chomsky, Noam. "Language and Unconscious Knowledge." In *Psychoanalysis and Language.* Ed. J. Smith. New Haven, CT: Yale University Press, 1978.
Copleston, Frederick. *A History of Medieval Philosophy.* London: Methuen & Co. Ltd.,1972.

———. *A History of Philosophy*. Vols. I-IV. Westminster, MD: The Newman Press, 1958.
Corbett, Lionel & Paul Kugler. "The Self in Jung and Kohut." *Dimensions of Self Experience*. Ed. A. Goldberg. Hillsdale, NJ: The Analytic Press, 1989.
Croce, Benedetto. *Aesthetic as Science of Expression and General Linguistic*. Tr. D. Ainslie. New York: Farrar, Straus, and Giroux, 1972.
Dawkins, Richard. *The Selfish Gene*. Oxford: Oxford University Press, 1976.
———. *Unweaving the Rainbow*. Boston: Mariner Books, 1998.
Deacon, Terrence W. *The Symbolic Species: The Co-Evolution of Language and the Brain*. New York: W. W. Norton & Co., 1997.
Dennett, Daniel C. *Darwin's Dangerous Idea: Evolution and the Meanings of Life*. New York: Simon & Schuster, 1995.
Derrida, Jacques. *A Derrida Reader: Between the Blinds*. Ed. P. Kamuf. New York: Columbia University Press, 1991.
———. *Of Grammatology*. Tr. G. C. Spivak. Baltimore, MD: The Johns Hopkins University Press, 1974.
Descartes, René. *Descartes: Philosophical Writings*. Tr. & ed. E. Anscombe & P. T. Geach. London: Thomas Nelson & Sons, 1954.
Downing, Christine. "Prologue." *Mirrors of the Self*. Los Angeles: J. P. Tarcher Publishing, 1991.
Dubois, Claude-Gilbert. *L'imaginaire de la Renaissance*. Paris: Presses Universitaires de France, 1985.
Durham, William. *Coevolution: Genes, Culture and Human Diversity*. Stanford, CA: Stanford University Press, 1991.
Edelson, Marshall. *Language and Interpretation in Psychoanalysis*. New Haven, CT: Yale University Press, 1975.
Fairbairn, W. Ronald D. *An Object-Relations Theory of Personality*. New York: Basic Books, 1954.
Fernandez, James W. "Reflections on Looking into Mirrors." *Semiotica* 30.1-2 (1980): 27-39.
Fordham, Michael. *Freud, Jung, Klein: The Fenceless Field: Essays on Psychoanalysis and Analytical Psychology*. Ed. R. Hobdell. London: Routledge, 1995.
Foucault, Michel. *Madness and Civilization: A History of Insanity in the Age of Reason*. Tr. R. Howard. London: Tavistock, 1967.
———. *The Order of Things: An Archaeology of the Human Sciences*. New York: Random House, 1970.
Freud, Anna. *The Ego and the Mechanisms of Defense*. New York: International Universities Press, 1946.
Freud, Sigmund. *The Origins of Psychoanalysis: Letters to Wilhelm Fliess, Drafts and Notes: 1892-1899*. Tr. E. Mosbacher & J. Strachey. New York: Basic Books, 1954.
———. *The Standard Edition of the Complete Psychological Works of Sigmund Freud*. 20 vols. Tr. J. Strachey. London: Hogarth Press, 1953-74.
———. *Totem and Taboo: Some Points of Agreement Between the Mental Lives of Savages and Neurotics*. Tr. J. Strachey. New York: W. W. Norton, & Co, 1950.
——— & Sándor Ferenczi. *The Correspondence of Sigmund Freud and Sándor Ferenczi, Volume 2: 1914-1919*. Eds. E. Falzeder & E. Brabant. Tr. P. T. Hoffer. Cambridge, MA: Harvard University Press, 1996.

Frey-Rohn, Liliane. *Friedrich Nietzsche*. Einsiedeln: Daimon Verlag, 1988.
Fuss, Diana. *Essentially Speaking: Feminism, Nature and Difference*. New York: Routledge, Kegan & Paul, 1989.
Giegerich, Wolfgang. *The Soul's Logical Life: Towards a Rigorous Notion of Psychology*. Frankfurt am Main: Peter Lang, 1998.
Goldberg, David Theo, ed. *Multiculturalism: A Critical Reader*. Oxford: Blackwell Publishers Ltd., 1994.
Gombrich, Ernst H. *The Story of Art*. London: Phaidon Press, 1972.
Grosskurth, Phyllis. *Melanie Klein: Her World and Her Work*. New York: Alfred A. Knopf, 1986.
Hamilton, William D. "The Evolution of Altruistic Behavior." *American Naturalist* 97 (1963): 354-56.
Hauke, Christopher. *Jung and the Postmodern: The Interpretation of Realities*. London: Routledge, 2000.
Havelock, Eric. *Preface to Plato*. Cambridge: Harvard University Press, 1963.
Heidegger, Martin. *Identity and Difference*. Tr. J. Stambaugh. New York: Harper and Row, 1969.
———. *Kant and the Problem of Metaphysics*. Tr. J. S. Churchill. Bloomington, IN: Indiana University Press, 1962.
———. *The End of Philosophy*. Tr. J. Stambaugh. New York: Harper & Row, Publishers, 1973.
Hendricks-Jansen, Horst. *Catching Ourselves in the Act: Situated Activity, Interactive Emergence, Evolutiuon, and Human Thought*. Cambridge, MA: MIT Press, 1996.
Hillman, James. *The Myth of Analysis: Three Essays in Archetypal Psychology*. Evanston, IL: Northwestern University Press, 1972.
Hogenson, George. "The Baldwin Effect: A Neglected Influence on C. G. Jung's Evolutionary Thinking." *The Journal of Analytical Psychology* 46.4 (2001): 591-611.
Hughes, Judith M. *Reshaping the Psychoanalytic Domain: The Works of Melanie Klein, W. R. D. Fairbairn & D. W. Winnicott*. Berkeley, CA: University of California Press, 1989.
Hume, David. *A Treatise of Human Nature*. Oxford: Oxford University Press, 1888/1976.
Hutchins, Edwin & Brian Hazelhurst. "Learning in the Cultural Process." *Artificial Life II: Proceedings of the Workshop on the Synthesis and Simulation of Living Systems, Santa Fe, 1990*. Eds. C. G. Langton, C. Taylor, J. D. Farmer, & S. Rasmussen. Redwood City, CA: Addison-Wesley, 1992.
Jacobson, Edith. *Depression: Comparative Studies of Normal, Neurotic, and Psychotic Conditions*. New York: International Universities Press, 1971.
———. *Psychotic Conflict and Reality*. New York: International Universities Press, 1967.
———. *The Self and the Object World*. New York: International Universities Press, 1964.
Jung, C. G.. *C. G. Jung Letters, Vol. I: 1906-1950*. Ed. G. Adler. Tr. R. F. C Hull. Bollingen Series XCV:1. Princeton, NJ: Princeton University Press, 1973.
———. *Memories, Dreams, Reflections*. Ed. Aniela Jaffé. Tr. R. & C. Winston, rev. ed. New York: Vintage Books, 1963.
———. *Nietzsche's Zarathustra: Notes of the Seminar given in 1934-1939*. Ed. J. L. Jarrett. Bollingen Series XCIX. Princeton, NJ: Princeton University Press, 1988.
———. *Psyche and Symbol*. New York: Anchor Books, 1958.

———. *Psychology of the Unconscious: A Study of the Transformations and Symbolism of the Libido*. Tr. B. M. Hinkle. Orig. Ger. ed., 1912. Bollingen Series XX. Princeton: Princeton University Press, 1991.

———. *The Collected Works of C. G. Jung*. Eds. H. Read, M. Fordham, G. Adler, and Wm. McGuire. Tr. R. F. C. Hull. 20 vols. Bollingen Series XX Princeton: Princeton University Press, 1953-1979.

Jung C. G. & F. Riklin. "The Associations of Normal Subjects." *Studies in Word Association*. Tr. M. D. Eder. New York: Moffat, Yard & Co., 1919.

Kant, Immanuel. *Critique of Pure Reason*. London: Macmillan & Co., 1953.

Kearney, Richard. *The Wake of the Imagination*. Minneapolis, MN: University of Minneapolis Press, 1988.

Kernberg, Otto. "A Psychoanalytic Classification of Character Pathology." *Journal of the American Psychoanalytic Association* 18 (1971): 800-802.

———. *Aggression in Personality Disorders and Perversions*. New Haven, CT: Yale University Press, 1992.

———. *Borderline Conditions and Pathological Narcissism*. New York: Jason Aronson, 1975.

———. "Early Ego Integration and Object Relations." *Annals of the New York Academy of Sciences* 193 (1972): 233-247.

———. "New Developments in Psychoanalytic Object Relations Theory. Parts I and III Normal and Pathological Development." Presented to the American Psychoanalytic Association, Washington, D. C., 1971. (Unpublished.)

Kohut, Heinz. *The Analysis of the Self: A Systematic Approach to the Psychoanalytic Treatment of Narcissistic Personality Disorder*. New York: International University Press, 1971.

———. *The Restoration of the Self*. New York: International Universities Press, 1977.

Kugler, Paul. "Clinical Authority: Some Thoughts Out of Season." *Quadrant: The Journal of Contemporary Jungian Thought* 23.2 (1990): 81-85.

———. "Jacques Lacan: Post-Modern Depth Psychology and the Birth of the Self-Reflexive Subject." *The Book of the Self: Person, Pretext, and Process*. Eds. P. Eisendrath & J. Hall. New York: New York University Press, 1987.

———. *The Alchemy of Discourse: Image, Sound and Psyche*. Rev. ed. Zürich: Daimon Verlag, 2002.

———. "The 'Subject' of Dreams." *Dreaming: Journal of the Association for the Study of Dreams* 3.2 (1993): 123-136.

———. "The Unconscious in a Postmodern Depth Psychology." *C. G. Jung and the Humanities*. Eds. K. Barnaby & P. Acierno. Princeton, NJ: Princeton University Press, 1990.

Lacan, Jacques. *Ecrits*. Tr. A. Sheridan. New York: W. W. Norton & Co., 1977.

———. "*Le Symbolique, l'Imaginaire et le Réel.*" Conférence à la Société Française de Psychanalyse. July 8, 1953 (unpublished).

———. "*Sur un Terrain en Friche*: Liminal Note." Lecture delivered at Johns Hopkins University, 1966. Transcribed and translated by R. Macksey. In *Lacan and Narration*. Ed. R. C. Davis. Baltimore: Johns Hopkins University Press, 1983.

———. *The Four Fundamental Concepts of Psychoanalysis*. Tr. A. Sheridan. New York: W. W. Norton & Co., 1978.

———. "The Insistence of the Letter in the Unconscious." *Structuralism*. Ed. J. Ehrman. New York: Anchor Books, 1970.

Lakoff, George & Mark Johnson. *Metaphors We Live By*. Chicago: University of Chicago Press, 1980.

Latour, Bruno. "The Historicity of Things," *Pandora's Hope: Essays on the Reality of Social Sciences*. Cambridge, MA: Harvard University Press, 1999,

Lévi-Strauss, Claude. *Structural Anthropology*. New York: Anchor Books, 1967.

Mahler, Margaret S. *The Selected Papers of Margaret S. Mahler, Vol. I: Infantile Psychosis and Early Contributions*. New York: Jason Aronson, 1979.

———, Fred Pine, & Anni Bergman, *The Psychological Birth of the Human Infant*. New York: Basic Books, 1975.

Mancia, Mauro & Luigi Longhin. "Kant's Philosophy and its Relationship with the Thought of Bion and Money-Kryle." *International Journal of Psychoanalysis* 81.6 (2000): 1197-1211.

Melchior-Bonnet, Sabine. *The Mirror: A History*. Tr. K. H. Jewett. New York: Routledge, 2001.

Miller, David L. *Hells and Holy Ghosts: A Theopoetics of Christian Belief*. New Orleans: Spring Journal Books, 2004.

———. "Through a Looking Glass: The World as Enigma." *Eranos 55-1986*. Frankfurt am Main: Insel Verlag, 1988.

Mitchell, Stephen & Margaret Black. *Freud and Beyond*. New York: Basic Books, 1995.

Mithen, Steven. *The Prehistory of the Mind*. London: Thames & Hudson, 1996.

Mogenson, Greg. *Greeting the Angels: An Imaginal View of the Mourning Process*. Amityville, NY: Baywood Publishing Co., 1992.

———. *The Dove in the Consulting Room: Hysteria and the Anima in Bollas and Jung*. Hove, UK: Brunner-Routledge, 2003.

Nietzsche, Friedrich. *The Gay Science*. In *The Portable Nietzsche*. Ed. and trans. W. Kaufmann. New York: Viking Press, 1968.

———. *Werke Grossoktavausgabe*. Vol. 3. Leipzig: Kroner, 1901.

Patterson, Richard. *Image and Reality in Plato's Metaphysics*. Indianapolis: Hackett Publishing, 1985.

Paz, Octavio. *The Bow and the Lyre*. Tr. R. Simms. New York: McGraw-Hill, 1975.

Pine, Fred. *Drive, Ego, Object, & Self: A Synthesis for Clinical Work*. New York: Basic Books, 1990.

———. *Diversity and Direction in Psychoanalytic Technique*. New Haven, CT: Yale University Press, 1998.

Pinker, Steven. *How the Mind Works*. New York: W. W. Norton, 1997.

———. *The Blank Slate: The Modern Denial of Human Nature*. New York: Viking Press, 2002.

———. *The Language Instinct*. New York: HarperCollins, 1994.

Plato. *The Republic*. Tr. D. Lee. Harmondsworth, UK: Penguin Classics, 1955.

Resnik, Salomon. *L'esperienza psicotica*. Turin: Bollati Boringhieri, 1986.

———. *Spazio mentale: sette lezioni alla Sorbona*. Turin: Bollati Boringhieri, 1990.

Richard of St. Victor. *De Unione Corporis et Spiritus*. In *Patrologia Latina*, 177, 285a-289a.

Richards, Robert J. *Darwin and the Emergence of Evolutionary Theories of Mind*. Chicago: University of Chicago Press, 1987.

Richetti, John. *Philosophical Writing: Locke, Berkeley, Hume.* Cambridge, MA: Harvard University Press, 1983.
Ricoeur, Paul. *Time and Narrative.* Chicago: University of Chicago Press, 1984.
Romanyshyn, Robert. *Psychological Life: From Science to Metaphor.* Austin, TX: University of Texas Press, 1982.
Rudnytsky, Peter L. *Reading Psychoanalysis: Freud, Rank, Ferenczi, Groddeck.* Ithaca, NY: Cornell University Press, 2002.
——, ed. *The Psychoanalytic Vocation: Rank, Winnicott, and the Legacy of Freud.* New Haven, CT: Yale University Press, 1991.
Samuels, Andrew. *Jung and the Post-Jungians.* London: Routledge & Kegan Paul, 1985.
——. *The Plural Psyche: Personality, Morality and the Father.* London: Routledge & Kegan Paul, 1989.
Schafer, Roy. *A New Language for Psychoanalysis.* New Haven, CT: Yale University Press, 1976.
Schoenewolf, Gerald. *Turning Points in Analytic Therapy: From Winnicott to Kernberg.* Northvale, NJ: Jason Aronson, 1990.
Serrano, Miguel. *C. G. Jung and Hermann Hesse: A Record of Two Friendships.* Tr. F. MacShane. New York: Schocken Books, 1968.
Shamdasani, Sonu. *Jung and the Making of Modern Psychology: The Dream of a Science.* Cambridge, UK: Cambridge University Press, 2003.
——. "Psychologies as Ontology-Making Practices: William James and the Pluralities of Psychological Experience." In *William James and the Varieties of Religious Experience.* Eds. J. Carrette, R. Morris, & T. Sprigge. London: Routledge, 2002.
Shorter, Edward. *From Paralysis to Fatigue: A History of Psychosomatic Illness in the Modern Era.* New York: The Free Press, 1992.
Smith, Joseph H., ed. "Introduction." *Psychoanalysis and Language.* New Haven, CT: Yale University Press, 1978.
Snell, Bruno. *Discovery of the Mind.* New York: Dover Publications, 1982.
Sokolowski, Robert. "Fiction and Illusion in David Hume's Philosophy." *The Modern Schoolman* 45 (1968): 189-225.
Soyland, A. John. *Psychology as Metaphor.* London: Sage Publications, 1994.
Spence, Donald. *The Freudian Metaphor.* New York: W. W. Norton & Co., 1987.
Spitz, René A. "Hospitalism: An Inquiry into the Genesis of Psychiatric Conditions of Early Childhood." *The Psychoanalytic Study of the Child.* Ed. R. S. Eissler. Vol. I. New York: International Universities Press, 1945.
——"Hospitalism: A Follow-up Report on the Investigation Described in Volume I." *The Psychoanalytic Study of the Child.* Ed. R. S. Eissler. Vol. II. New York: International Universities Press, 1946.
——. *The First Year of Life.* New York: International Universities Press, 1965.
Stern, Daniel. *The Interpersonal World of the Infant.* New York: Basic Books, 1985.
Stevens, Anthony. *Archetypes: A Natural History of the Self.* New York: Quill Books, 1983.
——. *Ariadne's Clue: A Guide to the Symbols of Humankind.* Princeton, NJ: Princeton University Press, 1999.
—— & John Price. *Evolutionary Psychiatry: A New Beginning.* London: Routledge, 1996.
Teicholz, Judith. *Kohut, Loewald, and the Postmoderns: A Comparative Study of Self and Relationship.* Hillsdale, NJ: The Analytic Press, 1999.

Tooby, John & Leda Cosmides. "On the Universality of Human Nature and the Uniqueness of the Individual: The Role of Genetics and Adaptation." *Journal of Personality* 58.1 (1990): 17-67.

——. "The Past Explains the Present: Emotional Adaptations and the Structure of Ancestral Environments." *Ethology and Sociobiology* 11 (1990): 375-424.

Turvey, Michael T. & Peter N. Kugler. *Information, Natural Law, and the Self-Assembly of Rhythmic Movement*. Hillsdale, NJ: Erlbaum Associates, 1987.

Warnock, Mary. *Imagination*. Berkeley, CA: University of California Press, 1976.

Wimsatt, William K. & Monroe C. Beardsley. *Literary Criticism: A Short History*. Lexington, KY: University of Kentucky Press, 1957.

Winnicott, Donald W. "Mirror-Role of Mother and Family in Child Development." *Playing and Reality*. Harmondsworth, UK: Penguin Books, 1971.

Wittgenstein, Ludwig. *Philosophical Investigations*. Tr. G. E. M. Anscombe. New York: Macmillan & Co., 1958.

Index

A

abuse, sexual xv
Adams, Michael
 xii, 49, 51, 132
Adler, Gerald 56, 102
anima 124, 125
Aquinas, St. Thomas 6
archetypal psychology xi
archetype
 xiii, 15, 16, 24, 31, 86, 101,
 105, 132, 137, 139, 142, 143
Aristotle 5, 67, 95, 103
Augustine, St. 6

B

Baldwin Effect 138–139
Baldwin, James Mark 139
Balint, Michael 48
Barthes, Roland 32, 33, 68
Baudelaire, Charles 13
Beardsley, Monroe C. 28, 29
Benjamin, Jessica 73
Bergman, Anni 52
Bible, King James Version of 115
biology, human
 in the development of psychic
  structure xvi, 131
 interaction with language and
  culture 131
Black, Margaret 45
Blackmore, Susan 137, 140
Blake, William 13
Bollas, Christopher xi, 41

Bonaventure, St. 6
borderline personality disorder
 54, 55
Bowlby, John 48
Brooks, Cleanth 29
Browne, Angela 100
Bruno, Giordano 8–9
Buie, Dan H. 56
Bundy, Murray W. 3
Byron, Lord George Gordon Noel
 13

C

Charcot, Jean-Martin 89
Chaucer, Geoffrey 114
Chomsky, Noam 16, 24
Coleridge, Samuel Taylor 13
complexes
 59, 76, 80, 99, 101,
 105, 116, 120, 121
Copernicus 8, 69
Copleston, Frederick 3, 6
Corbett, Lionel 57, 142
Cosmides, Leda 136
Croce, Benedetto 5

D

Darwin, Charles 134, 143
Dawkins, Richard 136, 143
Deacon, Terrence W. 131, 137
deconstruction 18, 32, 33
Dennett, Daniel C.
 136, 138, 139

Derrida, Jacques 18–19, 33, 69, 132
Descartes, René xiv, 9–10, 67–68, 71
developmental psychology xi
Downing, Christine 72
drive theory
    xiv, 14, 32, 34, 41, 43, 54, 57–58, 78, 104
DSM-III 55
DSM-IV 105
Durham, William 137

E

Edelson, Marshall 57
ego xv, 43, 47, 48, 50, 71, 74, 80, 81, 92
    development of 46, 54
ego psychology xi, 16, 42, 43–45
ego/self structure 73–75, 76, 82, 134
Elijah 118
epistemology 13, 35, 103
evolution xvi, 131, 135

F

Fairbairn, W. Ronald D. 48, 49
false memory syndrome xv, 86
fantasy 17, 70, 86, 92–93, 97, 104, 126
Federn, Paul 51
Ferenczi, Sándor 42
Fernandez, James W. 72
Fichte, Johann Gottlieb 13
Ficino, Marsilio 8
Finkelhor, David 100
Fliess, Wilhelm 90
Flournoy, Theodore 113
Fordham, Michael xii, 49
Foucault, Michel 18, 67, 68, 132

free association 44, 98
Freud, Anna 43, 47, 48
Freud, Sigmund 102
    analysis of 42
    broken male friendships of 50
    development of theories of 23, 41–43
    ego development in theory of 46
    ego in the psychology of 43
    fear of the dead in theory of 117
    primacy of sexuality in theory of 16
    seduction theory of 88–92
    theoretical conflict with Jung 49
    theory of imaging of 14, 70
    view of libido in theory of 51
    view of the unconscious in theory of 24–25

G

Gandhi, Mohandas K. 118
ghosts 116–118
Giegerich, Wolfgang 72
God, existence of 120
Goodheart, William 105
Groddeck, Georg 42
Grosskurth, Phyllis 47
Guntrip, Harry 48

H

Hamilton, William 134
Hartmann, Heinz 44, 55
Hauke, Christopher xii, 132
Hazelhurst, Brian 140
Hegel, Georg Wilhelm Friedrich 33, 71, 72
Heidegger, Martin 8, 71
Heisenberg, Werner 143

INDEX

Hendricks-Jansen, Horst 140
Hillman, James 58, 115
Hinton, Geoffrey 140
Hogenson, George
   137, 139, 140, 142, 143
Holy Ghost 114–115
Homer 114
Hughes, Judith M. 49
Hugo of St. Victor 6
Hugo, Victor 13
Hume, David 10–12
Hutchins, Edwin 140

I

id 43
id psychology xi, 14, 16, 41–43, 46, 50, 54–55, 70, 93
identity theory 43
image, psychic
  and biological experience 134
  as mediator between idea and thing 20, 76
  as representation of drives 70, 105
  evolution in Western thought 3–20
  marginalization of xiii
  of the dead xvi, 116
  relationship to personal history xv, 86, 87, 105
imago 69, 96
  as merger between perception and apperception 97
  as reflection of dreamer's inner world 76
  parental 116, 120
Industrial Revolution 13
International Psychoanalytic Association 48

J

Jacobson, Edith 50–52, 52, 55, 56
Jewett, K. H. 72
Johnson, Mark 37
Jung, Carl Gustav
  analysis of Freud 42
  concept of imago of 69
  concept of psychic reality of 17, 49
  concept of the self in psychology of 71
  conflict with Sigmund Freud 49
  death of father 112
  dream interpretation by 76–77
  emphasis on mother in psychology of 49
  function of the archetype in the theories of 31
  function of the unconscious in theories of 31
  images of the dead in the psychology of 111–112
  influence upon New Critics of theories of 29
  symbolism in theories of 24
  theoretical differences with Freud in theory of 50
  theory of role of memories in neurosis of 94
  treatment of severely disturbed patients by 51
  view of imaging of 14, 16, 20, 70, 116
  Word Association Experiments of 44
Jung, Emma 124

K

Kant, Immanuel 12–14, 76–77
Kearney, Richard 3, 10
Keats, John 13
Kernberg, Otto 53–56, 105
Khidr 25, 26, 27
Kierkegaard, Søren 14
Klein, Melanie xii, 47, 49
Klein, Milton 90
Klein-Jung hybrid xii, 49
Kohut, Heinz
    xiv, 53, 55, 57, 74–75, 105
Koran 25
Krafft-Ebing, Richard von 113
Kugler, Paul
    xiv, 30, 31, 57, 58, 63, 74, 132, 133, 134, 142
Kugler, Peter N. 143

L

Lacan, Jacques
    xiv, xv, 27, 32, 53, 57, 60, 61, 70, 72, 72–73, 105, 133, 134
Lakoff, George 37
Lamarck, Jean-Baptiste 139, 140
Langs, Robert J. 105
language
    acquisition of 62–63, 73, 79–82, 131, 134, 142
    as metaphor 37
    function of 30, 141
    interaction with biology of 132–143
    limitations of 34, 36
    role in development of the psyche of xvi, 18–19, 68
    role in psychoanalytic theory of 32, 57
Latour, Bruno 15, 16
Lévi-Strauss, Claude 30–31, 32
Locke, John 10
Lowenstein, Rudolph M. 55

M

Magritte, René 96
Mahler, Margaret 50, 51, 55
Malek-Nasrie, Gitta 102
Masson, Jeffrey M. 90, 91
Melchior-Bonnet, Sabine 72
meme 140
memory
    Jung's view of function of 94
    nature of 96
    nature of in theories of Freud 93
    of childhood seduction 87
Miller, Alice 90
Miller, David L. 72, 114, 117
mimetic function 133
mirror stage 60–63
Mitchell, Stephen 45
Mithen, Steven 137
Modernist School of literary theory 28–29, 68
Moebius strip 126
Mogenson, Greg xi, 116
Morgan, Conway L. 139–140
Moses 25
multiculturalism xii
multiple personality disorder 86
Myers, F. W. H. 113

N

narcissistic personality disorder 55, 56
Nasrudin, Mullah 102
Neolithic period 136

Nerval, Gérard de 13
New Criticism 29
Newton, Isaac 105
Nietzsche, Friedrich
  14, 33, 34–35, 68, 106
Nowlan, Steven 140

O

object relations theory
  xi, 16, 48, 53, 104, 105
Oedipus complex
  xiv, 14, 41, 43, 48, 93, 94, 101
onto-theology, medieval
  xiii, 4, 6, 7, 8, 13, 19
ontology 6, 102–103, 134
Osborn, H. F. 139

P

Paracelsus 8
Paz, Octavio 60
personality, construction of 58
physics 121
Piaget, Jean 5, 24
Pine, Fred xi, 44, 48, 52
Pinker, Steven 131, 136, 140
Plato 4, 67, 95, 103, 138
Pleistocene period 136
Plotinus 6
Porphyry 6
Price, John 136, 137
Prince, Morton 112
Proclus 6
psyche 74, 81, 132
psychoanalysis
  history of xiv
  theories of 103

R

Rank, Otto 42
Rappaport, David 55

realism 37
relational psychology 16, 43
Remus, Uncle 102
revenants 116
Riklin, F. 44
Rudnytsky, Peter L. 42, 43

S

Salome 118
Samuels, Andrew xi
Saussure, Ferdinand de 30
Schafer, Roy 57
Schelling, Friedrich Wilhelm
  Joseph von 13
Schoenewolf, Gerald
  51, 53, 55
Scholasticism xv, 9, 68
Schrödinger, Erwin 143
Searles, Harold Frederic 105
self 50, 71, 74, 81–
  82, 86, 142
  in contemporary Freudian
    psychology xiv
  infant's development of sense of
    51, 52
  Jung's concept of 71
self psychology xi, xv, 16, 55–58
self-reflection 58–63
semiology 30
Serrano, Miguel 71
Shakespeare, William 114
Shamdasani, Sonu 15, 50
Shelley, Percy Bysshe 13
Shorter, Edward 28
somnambulism 112
Sophocles 114
Soyland, A. John 37
space-time continuum 121
Spence, Donald 37, 45
spirits, as unconscious complexes
  120

Spitz, Réne A. 45, 51, 56
splitting 55, 56, 86, 89
Stern, Daniel 73, 74
Stevens, Anthony
    136, 137, 140
Stone, L. 55
Strachey, James 91
Structuralism 30–31
superego
    42, 44, 46, 48, 52, 59

T

tabula rasa 10
Teicholz, Judith 132
time, experience of 127
Tooby, John 136
transference 57, 86, 91
trauma 86, 89, 94, 100–101
Turvey, Michael T. 143
typology 101–102

U

unconscious xiii–xiv, 86, 93–94
  as the underworld 115
  difficulty of defining 27
  in theories of Carl Jung 31
  in theories of Claude Lévi-
    Strauss 31
  in theories of Jean Piaget 24
  in theories of Noam Chomsky
    24
  in theories of Sigmund Freud
    23–24

W

Wallon, Henri 71, 72, 73
Wimsatt, William K. 28, 29
Winnicott, Donald
    48, 61, 72, 105

Wittgenstein, Ludwig 132
Word Association Experiments
    44

Z

Zola, Emile 126